Tackling THE Taxman

How to Keep the CRA from Controlling Your Investments and Your Life

ALEX DOULIS

ECW PRESS

Published by ECW PRESS
2120 Queen Street East, Suite 200, Toronto, Ontario, Canada M4E 1E2

LIBRARY AND ARCHIVES CANADA CATALOGUING IN PUBLICATION

Doulis, Alex
Tackling the taxman : how to keep the CRA from controlling your investments
and your life : a tax empowerment guide / Alex Doulis.

ISBN 1-55022-734-3

1. Tax planning — Canada — Popular works. 2. Income tax — Canada —
Popular works. 3. Finance, Personal — Canada. 1. Title.

HJ4661.D68 2006   336.24'2'0971   C2005-907234-2

Cover and text design: Tania Craan
Production: Mary Bowness
Printing: Transcontinental

This book is set in AGaramond

With the publication of *Tackling the Taxman* ECW PRESS acknowledges the generous
financial support of the Government of Canada through the Book Publishing Industry
Development Program (BPIDP), the Canada Council for the Arts, and the Ontario Arts
Council, for our publishing activities.

Canada   Canada Council   Conseil des Arts
           for the Arts   du Canada

DISTRIBUTION

CANADA: Jaguar Book Group, 100 Armstrong Ave., Georgetown, ON L7G 5S4

PRINTED AND BOUND IN CANADA

ECW PRESS
ecwpress.com

In this book, I often refer to the Canada Revenue Agency (CRA) by its old and still commonly used informal name of Revcan. I know that the new name has a warmer, friendlier feel to it, but it is still the same old bunch. Why they gave up a brand name that everyone cowered at the sight or sound of I'll never understand. Perhaps some party supporter of a cabinet minister had a printing company ready to sell them new stationery.

This book is my fourth foray into the Canadian finance system. The first two — *Take Your Money and Run* and *My Blue Haven* — dealt with creative but totally legal ways to shift your money offshore and out of the greedy grasp of the taxman. The third — *The Bond's Revenge* — explained the intricacies of the corporate bond market and a way to invest in which the corporation had to pay you for the use of your money.

The book you have in your hands examines how the existing tax system in Canada functions and the abuses it generates. It shows you how your tax department bends the rules it creates to take advantage of the taxpayer and how the decrease in its powers as a result of court action is leading to desperation. To eliminate the abuses of the tax system by government, we need to take the tax system away from the politicians, who use it as a tool to punish their opponents and reward their friends.

Of course, I write with a measure of bitterness, having had some dealings with Revcan over my now extensive lifetime. But along with that, I write as one with an extensive professional background in investing and tax matters.

After ten years as a geologist, I spent twenty years in the financial industry as a chartered financial analyst. Initially, I put my geological bona fides to work and was a mining analyst. I went on from there to become a partner in Gordon Capital and a director of and partner in McNeil Mantha. I continue to advise portfolio investors through Liberty Consulting.

From 1990 to the present, I put my advice into practice and lived outside Canada, spending a good part of every year plying the Mediterranean and the Atlantic in my yacht and researching and writing the aforementioned books.

Now I am back in the Magical Kingdom of Canada. I have two aims in my dwindling years: first, to be a scourge to all the eminently deserving lads and lasses of Revcan, and second, to be of aid to you in your own dance with the devil. It is my hope that when you finish reading this book you will no longer cower like most Canadians at the mere mention of the name Canada Revenue Agency. You will know what your rights are and what legal steps to take before the taxman comes calling audit demand in hand.

INTRODUCTION

I do not offer accounting or legal advice in this book; rather, I inform you how Revcan works and what you can do to protect yourself when the tax beast gets vicious. I'm going to use the case study method employed by business schools because you, as an individual conducting your business of living and working, will recognize at some point that the highest-cost item of your business[1] is taxes. You will become aware of the pitfalls of rules. Revcan likes to work with rules rather than laws. Rules depend on who is imposing them and on whom they are being imposed.

[1] You may also conclude, as I did while operating the business of being Alex Doulis, that you are a minority shareholder in your own enterprise.

Precedents don't count when rules are being exercised. Let me give you an example.

There was a case in the 1950s where a Newfoundland merchant mariner had been at sea for more than five years, never setting foot in Canada. When he returned, Revcan went after him for back taxes. His defence was that he hadn't resided in Canada for the five years in question. Revcan's argument was that he hadn't established a new residence and therefore was *resident in the last place of permanent residency.* His last permanent residence was Canada. Revcan prevailed.

Well, that was a good rule for Revcan until in recent years people have left Canada for a multitude of reasons. Some of these individuals established a residency in another country, worked there, and then went on extended holidays, giving up their most recent residency. Some who returned were then told by Revcan that, seeing as for a period they had no permanent residency, they were by default residents of Canada.

What happened to that ruling about people with no current residency being resident in their last country of residence? Without a lawyer to find that and plead it in court for $50,000, it becomes of little help to the man or woman on the street.

"But wait," you say, "a government department wouldn't act dishonestly."

A government department? Maybe not. But we are talking money here, and as you know there are those who will lie, cheat, steal, and kill for the filthy lucre. What is even more frightening is that I will tell you of the abuse of citizens through the vast powers of audit by tax-collecting civil servants that could be repeated by agencies such as our counterspies. They have been given excessive powers to combat terrorism that, if misused as the tax department has misused audits, will make Stalin's Russia look like a day care. Enemies of the ruling party will be crushed, with no judicial recourse to defend themselves.

For years on my website, I have had a page where taxpayers could report their horror stories to prepare for this book. Most of what you will read came from that page. Some of what you will read came from my own experience.

In all of the cases, I, as the author, provide notes about how to avoid the pitfall in the case. These are the real meat of the sandwich and should be remembered for future use should a situation arise for you similar to the one discussed.

How is this for a job description? You go to people and demand that they give you money. They are reluctant, but you tell them that it's going to be used for their benefit and that actually, like a Ponzi scheme, they will get more out of the deal than what they put in. Then, after you've collected and given the money to your boss, you see in the newspaper that the guys you handed the money to have been doling it out to their friends and lovers, while the services that were promised to the payers are not forthcoming. How well do you think you are going to be received the next time you come by with your demands for payment?

That in a nutshell describes income tax in Canada. A portion of the funds collected is passed out to party supporters as cash or positions. Think of all the boards, consuls, and positions doled out to the party faithful. Think about a six-month wait for heart surgery. That redistribution of Canadians' wealth from the middle class to the party faithful has been going on since 1917 in Canada.

If you are working at CRA, you are being driven to bring in the cash, while the donors are working to diminish their taxable income (tax avoidance — an economic necessity)[2] or hide their income (tax evasion — a criminal act). You are constantly being pushed for performance while your superiors remind you incessantly of the constraints of the *Tax Operation Manual*, the Charter of Rights and Freedoms, and the Income Tax Act. The tax collectors are told to go forth and rape, loot, and pillage while standing on one foot, with their hands tied behind their backs, blindfolded. I have seen a high burn-out rate in collections and auditing at Revcan.

The question naturally arises: how do employees survive in that kind of environment? Well, every now and then, they put the elevated foot down and slip out of their bonds and blindfolds. *Tax Operation Manuals* are quietly moved to the bottom drawer, and the pages of the Income Tax Act imposing limits are torn out. The start of a new day!

However, as with all illegal undertakings, violations of the Income Tax Act by anyone, including CRA employees, often get exposed. When a tax-paying individual violates the act, you'll see the event highly publicized, particularly if it is a person of some renown. In fact, if you are of high enough public profile, CRA will either pursue you or con-

---

[2] In 1938, during a landmark case in the House of Lords in England, Lord Curzon ruled in *Westminster v. Regina* that "a man had the right to arrange his financial affairs in such a manner as to attract the least amount of tax." Canada was a dominion of Britain at the time, and the ruling thus applies in Canada. Interestingly, Oliver Wendell Holmes ruled similarly in the U.S. Supreme Court in 1929. These cases established the legality of tax avoidance.

nect you to a third-party violation of the tax code for the sheer publicity value even if you are uninvolved in the fraud. I will show you two such instances in this book.

When a Revcan employee such as Nicola Robichaud, Gordon MacDonald, or Art Payne slips up and violates the *Tax Operation Manual* or the Income Tax Act, do we see a banner headline in his or her hometown newspaper? Nope.

I've often wondered what happens in the local CRA office after the expenditure of tens of thousands of dollars on a lost legal case and the attendant embarrassment. Is it treated like the unofficial national sport, hockey? The other team members come by in the locker room (read office) and try to cheer up their downcast colleague. "Nice shot on goal, Art. Shame about the goalkeeper and the defencemen getting in the way" — the goalkeeper obviously being the judge and the defencemen the opposing lawyers. Do they move Art down to the minor league? Send him off to perform audits in Come by Chance, Newfoundland?

I don't know. However, in all the readings I've done, I have yet to find a repeat offender violating the act while employed by Revcan. At some level, I suspect, the Department of National Revenue does look down on these lapses by its employees. That doesn't mean, however, that employees having seen their colleagues slip off the wagon are going to take the event to heart and pledge solemnly to maintain the Act once again.

No, Income Tax Act violations by government employees are like SARS. Once in the system, they spread like wildfire, jumping from office to office and filling the courts with complainants.

How do the tax collectors slip the ties that bind? First, you'll find in this book that the most common and destructive device is the mixing of information from an audit with that of an investigation, which are different activities. Second, lying is way up there, to the extent that a victorious lawyer, having protected a client, wondered, for public consumption, why taxpayers were required to be honest and not tax collectors.

Has this ever happened to you? There you are at the breakfast table on a February morning reading the local paper. Once again (just before tax time) you see a story of the local doctor/lawyer/whomever who got busted by Revcan. He or she was exposed for having underreported or hidden income. Or maybe it was inflated expenses or nonexistent deductions. Whatever it was, it didn't get past the ever-vigilant eye of Revcan. Often you aren't told when this event occurred. It may even have been a few years ago.

Have you ever wondered why you seldom see those news reports in the middle of summer? The reason is that the story might not get seen (holidays, summer cottaging, whatever), and there is the need to have the message out when it can have an impact.[3] That's because there is a subliminal message in that news release: "Don't even think of trying to cheat us." The message is more effective if conveyed just at tax time, when it will discourage the already wary.

Another question. When was the last time your morning paper had a story about local David slaying Goliath, the tax monster? The story of the victorious tax-paying David overcoming the rapacious tax collector will seldom if ever make it into your local paper, and if it does it won't be at tax time. Why? First, because the taxpayer doesn't have a press department working on his image trying to influence

[3] See *Manufacturing Consent,* by Edward S. Herman.

public opinion. Second, because Revcan *does* have a publicity machine and doesn't like that kind of story hitting the streets, particularly when it's harvest time.

There is more. An individual fighting a tax case will often plead it in the Federal Tax Court. The come-on is that it is cheaper, faster, et cetera than going to one of those expensive, drawn-out, real courts. The net result is that in Tax Court Revcan wins most of the time. In the real court, the taxpayer wins most often. But who goes to the real courts? Not individuals but corporations. After they have been convicted and tried in Tax Court, the corporations head off to a real court. For them, the legal fees are a tax deductible expense. If they win, they have their tax benefit and can write off the costs. However, what they won't get is a judgment that has the government paying the costs.[4]

Individual taxpayers rarely go to a real court because doing so will cost them upward of $50,000 in legal fees, which aren't deductible, and there is little possibility that the crown will be forced to pay costs. It is a fabulous no-lose situation for the taxman. A taxpayer faced with a tax bill for $10,000 that he knows is improper will, when faced with the costs to defend his position, fold. In one important case, you will read about the tax collectors who went after people too poor to be able to afford an accountant, never mind a lawyer. The taxpayer killed herself. That is serious folding. You may not believe that the taxman can kill you, but I will tell you of another case where, after the dance with the taxers started, my client died of a heart attack within months.

---

[4] There is a famous case you'll read about where the government acted so badly that the judge awarded costs to the defendant. As well, there is now before the courts a case to award costs to the taxpayer where Revcan actions reduced the amount of money it was scheduled to collect.

In the Scandinavian countries, where tax rates often exceed sixty percent, there is little tax evasion or avoidance because people perceive they are getting fair value for their tax dollars. In Canada, the litany of tax waste on cabinet members' girlfriends, cynical gun registries, and government advertising while the medical care system cries out for funding is leading taxpayers astray.

In some areas, such as convenience stores where the cash register never rings or the offshore where the wealthy move their stash, Revcan has thrown in the towel with regard to enforcement since the cost of collection is excessive. Therefore, it must get tougher with the remaining taxpayers. Should you be abused, your member of Parliament will be of no help to you since he is as afraid of Revcan as you are. As well, he's the guy who gets the money, so he has little interest in interceding on your behalf when the boys and girls at the tax office go off the deep end.

Well, it gets even more curious, as you are about to see.

CHAPTER 1

An Emergency MEASURE

THE FEDS' EXCUSE FOR IMPOSING INCOME TAX

The Canada Revenue Agency (CRA) is charged with the responsibility of collecting from the citizens the amount of money needed to run the country. Notice I didn't say corporations, since they pay no tax. Their tax is a cost of doing business passed on to the consumer. Obviously, extracting money from people who can see little in the way of tangible benefits from their donations to the federal government coffers makes CRA's job very difficult. To make things worse, the press is full of stories of political cheerleaders living high off the hog or receiving questionable payments. One of the problems is that our tax system is upside down. We should pay taxes to the city based on our ability to pay, and that government should then dole out funds to the next levels of government as it sees fit. The cities might even find one level of government superfluous and stop funding it. So how did we get to this ridiculous situation? It wasn't by design.

The founding fathers of Canada in the British North America Act and the associated documents provided that the right of direct taxation rested with the provinces. After all, it was the provinces that were confederating, and they had the taxing power to begin with. As well, they were the source of services and infrastructure in 1860s Canada. In those days, the provinces resembled city states in that there were one or two large towns that needed financial administration and the rest was hinterland that no one cared about. Yes, the system was originally right side up.

The framers of Confederation didn't dismiss the federal government out of hand. They gave it the right to indirect taxation[5] such as customs and excise as well as the profit from the issuing of currency and coinage. What more could the federal government need?

I'm sure you are amazed that such a rational system could exist. The area in which funds were raised was the same area in which they were spent, and the people responsible for the raising and spending lived in the vicinity. You can imagine how difficult it was to slide some funds out of the tax pot for friends. The pot rested close to the contributors to it and was under their watchful eyes. No Sponsorship Scandal for them.

---

[5] The term "indirect taxation" refers to the fact that the individual does not pay the tax directly but finds it applied to some service or product that he then pays through acquisition of the product or service. Hence, liquor taxes are not direct taxes since they aren't levelled on the individual.

But no such Shangri-La can be allowed to continue indefinitely. What destroyed this one was the same as what has destroyed personal freedoms and civil liberties throughout history: the National Emergency! Governments will not stand by while they are threatened, and the Government of Great Britain was being threatened by the Huns. It was 1917, and more money was needed to fight a war to save the nation — not the nationals but the nation. There was little concern about ruining people's lives with an already horrendous tax known as conscription, where the state grabbed your male child and seldom gave him back in the same condition as it received him, if at all.

A *temporary emergency measure* was passed in 1917 allowing the Canadian federal government to impose an income tax on the people of Canada until such time as the war ended. The reason it had to be done as a temporary emergency measure is that it was illegal. Section 90 of the British North America Act allocated direct taxation to the provinces. Section 91 of the same act forbade the provinces from giving up any of their rights. Well, this was an emergency, and good patriots could overlook a little temporary rule bending until such time as the government was once again safe. Revcan has argued that included in the BNA Act was the clause that the federal government could raise money by any means, but direct taxation was reserved for the provinces. If this were not true, then why was the 1917 income tax legislation passed only as a temporary and emergency measure?

After the war ended, the Ottawa crowd realized that they now had power because they had the nation's wealth.

Put yourself in their position.[6] Would you have given up the power serendipity had put into your hands and become a figurehead once again?

It might have ended there with rates being low and the tax mostly a nuisance. But then we had another — you guessed it — National Emergency! The Nazis had killed off ninety percent of the gypsy population of Europe and were closing in on the remainder. Rates were hiked and the concept of "general coffers" refined. This latter mechanism allowed the government to put all the money it raised into one big pot. That way you don't know if the gasoline tax you pay is going into the roads or the health tax into the hospitals. If the citizen of the late 1990s wanted to dig hard enough, he would have found that the average personal contribution to general coffers was about $14,000, for which he received $2,000 in health care and about $3,000 in education. Gosh, there's $9,000 unaccounted for. How different it would be if Canadians were charged fourteen percent of their tax load for health and twenty percent for education and the amounts placed in specific accounts like the Canada Pension Plan. If the need for more health or education arose, then tax rates could be adjusted. But then the amounts raised for health could never be available for graft.

Speaking of which, general coffers combined with the expansion of the Canadian government to fight the National Emergency meant that many a new crown corporation, agency, consular office, et cetera were opened. When

---

[6] A similar situation arose after the Liberal win over the Conservatives in the 1990s. The Conservatives had introduced the hated Goods and Services Tax, which fell on every transaction in the country. The Liberals, sensing the antipathy to this tax, decided to campaign on eliminating it. Once in power and seeing the revenue-generating capability, the Liberals reneged on their promise to eliminate it.

the National Emergency was finally overcome, in place was a myriad of spending programs, not to mention political plums to be dished out. There was no one to set limits. Eventually, the spending became so bad that Canada was cast into deferred taxes. Under that system, the government borrows the money it currently spends with the understanding that taxpayers of the future will pay. Therefore, bonds were issued, redeemable well in the future when the current government would be long gone. At one point in the 1990s, thirty-five percent of every tax dollar collected went to pay the interest on the national debt (with no National Emergency to blame), and the foreign currency bonds of Canada were downgraded by the bond-rating agencies. The citizens were being told that all this money was being extracted so as to benefit them and that in reality tax rates were low. Well, yes, the current tax rate was low, but the economists and financial journalists disclosed that the government was spending fifty percent of the gross national product (GNP) while admitting to collecting only forty-five percent. That was a terrible event for government as the percent of GNP then became recognized as the actual tax burden that citizens had to pay.

Much of this was foreseen in 1969 by Edgar Benson, a finance minister who laid out a new national taxation system designed to increase fairness for the taxpayers and the tax collectors. In 1972, after due consideration, the government threw out the benefits for the taxpayers and adopted those for the tax collectors. There was an exodus of wealthy Canadians to the promised land — wherever that might be. This exodus diminished the tax base, and poorer Canadians were now called upon to belly up to the bar for our government. By the mid-1980s, the tax grab on the marginal dollar of income was in excess of fifty-five percent. The Capital Gains Tax had been changed so that losses could only be offset against gains rather than other income (Benson had declared that a dollar was a dollar irrespective of how earned, expended, or lost and should be taxed as such, but his successors didn't accept that). Car expenses were shaved. As a result, no cabinet minister had a car, only a constant chauffeur from the car pool, tax free. Attendance at conventions was limited for taxpayers, but MPS were given unlimited tax-free travel. MPS embraced tax avoidance as popes did Catholicism. It was their religion. No taxable frequent flyer points for them. Instead, they got free airline passes. Mistresses were being driven back and forth to Toronto[7] in government limousines seeing as there would be no tax deduction for the members' use of cars. Canada's military flew the country's politicians, families, and hangers on to the holiday spots of the world. As the strains of government spending started to bleed the health care system, the politicians established a private hospital for themselves just across the river from Ottawa in Hull, Quebec. There would be no waiting in line by our back-benchers. Canadians looking at their elected representatives' reluctance to accept taxable benefits realized that tax avoidance was the new National Emergency and rallied to the flag.

---

[7] Gib Parent, while speaker of the House, was at one time having to consult with a shapely young thing in Toronto about how to maintain proper decorum in the House. He would fly his "consultant" up to Ottawa on his wife's airline pass for weekenders while telling the wife in southern Ontario that he was working. She found out what he was working at and kicked him out of the house, maintaining custody of her airline pass. The parliamentarian was reduced to having to send a government limo for the bimbo. It was weekend work, and thus the taxpayers had to pay overtime for the bimbo limo.

This made Revcan's job even more difficult. Aside from people leaving with their assets, there was the wholesale movement of assets by Canadians to tax havens. The only way that the flow of funds could be maintained was to try to crack down on the use of tax havens. But not those that hurt the political class. While spying on every foreign movement of funds by Canadians, the Department of Finance changed the Income Tax Act to allow Canadians to own ships abroad and not pay taxes on the earnings of those ships. The ships didn't have to be built in Canada, crewed by Canadians, or registered in Canada. This was a tax gift to all the Bermudian[8] shipping magnates living in Canada. While Revcan was seeking to plug the hole in the financial dike that allowed billions to flee, the Department of Finance was blasting holes in the dikes big enough to float a Canadian steamship through (see Chapter 14). But the government made matters even more difficult for Revcan starting in the 1970s.

The governments of the 1970s and 1980s tried to use the tax system as an economic and social tool. We had special tax programs for scientific research[9] and moviemaking and God knows what. In the end, CRA saw that each of these programs allowed tax avoidance and tackled them strenuously. Here you had the absurd picture of Ottawa handing out tax shields and its handmaiden trying to close them down. In the 1980s, the federal Department of Finance

[8] At the time of this writing, there is only one known Bermudian shipping magnate in Canada, and he is the prime minister.

[9] I have concluded that politicians and cabinet ministers are avid readers of newspapers, and any mentioned weakness of the country in the press is immediately seen as an area for government largesse.

tried to squeeze every loophole shut so as to be able to cover its spending. The citizens saw helicopter scandals, Jane Stewart's $3 billion gaffe, $7 million consular offices in London, Paris, New York, and Los Angeles for failed politicians — and dug their heals in. This made CRA more vicious, but unlike the duke of Alba in sixteenth-century Holland they couldn't hang the reluctant taxpayer.

So now you have a government department collecting money probably illegally[10] from people who are becoming more disgusted with the uses to which their tax dollars are allocated. Pity the poor CRA employees. Here is what they have fallen to.

---

[10] *The Lord Nelson Hotel v. Regina* case of the 1950s in the Supreme Court of Canada basically upheld that the BNA Act was being violated by the current imposition of a federal income tax.

CHAPTER 2

The Four Horsemen
OF THE APOCALYPSE
....

AUDITS, INVESTIGATIONS, CONFIDENTIALITY,
AND COLLECTION

There are four major parts of the Income Tax Act that affect taxpayers. They are audit, investigation, confidentiality, and collection.

An audit is an examination of your financial affairs by Revcan to determine if you have paid the correct amount of tax. You are required to provide your financial records for the past taxation year and possibly the three previous ones. Third parties, including your lawyer and accountant, are required to provide information. It is supposed to be confidential and information passed only between you and the Revcan auditor. You'll see in the cases I provide that this rule isn't always respected.

Individuals often confuse an audit with an investigation.

There can be no criminal offence resulting from an audit. Therefore, there is no protection under the Charter of Rights and Freedoms during an audit. Client confidentiality for lawyers or accountants and their clients is suspended. This is an examination, not an investigation, and the information obtained is inadmissible in court, logically, because it was obtained without the protection of the Charter. In Canada, an audit will be conducted by an auditor, while an investigation is carried out by the Special Investigation Unit's (SIU) investigators. Obviously, when someone from Revcan shows up at the door, you want to see his or her business card to be sure you are talking to an auditor from whom you have nothing to fear except a reassessment upward in your taxes payable (there is seldom a downward revision, and when it arises it may be ignored).

While you are being audited, your taxpayer confidentiality must be respected. Your name cannot appear in the press, and none of the information can be discussed outside the precincts of the audit.

Quite differently, when an investigator arrives, he has as his objective the collection of enough information to convict you and send you to jail. You should never answer even the most innocent of questions from an investigator without legal advice. You can refuse to answer without legal representation. Once you are under investigation, the fact can be publicized if you have been charged, but not until then. The fact that you are being audited is confidential. By law, Revcan cannot reveal that you are being audited or have been audited.

The other question that people often ask me is "How was I chosen? Why was I chosen?" The reasons are manifold. The first category is a group that Revcan believes has the ability to hide income, the amounts of which could be significant. Typical are dentists, building contractors, and home repair providers. Another group consists of people who are "high-profile" Canadians. Such a person would have his name readily recognized by people in all or a large portion of the country. "Wait a minute," you say, "high profile? What has that got to do with tax collection?" Well, Revcan likes to get names you recognize, except politicians,[11] in the press to show you that all are fair game. The sort of thing it likes would be the following:

> **Dateline North Pole:** CRA in its relentless pursuit of tax cheats has begun prosecution of Mr. S. Claus (a.k.a. Santa). Over many years, Mr. Claus has been receiving cookies and milk on the evening of December 24. The defendant at no time reported this, claiming these were gifts freely given. CRA argued successfully in Federal Tax Court that these were benefits arising from his employment. Mr. Claus also argued that CRA had no jurisdiction as he, Mr. Claus, while residing at the North Pole was not a resident of Canada and therefore not liable for taxation in Canada. CRA produced a document for the Federal Tax Court judge showing that

---

[11] You may remember that there were accusations of suspicious cash payment being made to a former prime minister, Brian Mulroney. The author, William Kaplan, describes how the former prime minister would meet in hotel rooms with Karlheinz Schrieber to receive envelopes stuffed with cash in the amounts of $100,000 to $300,000. Instead of having Revcan investigate the financial affairs of this ex-PM, it was decided to have the RCMP, who are much less skilled in this area, look into the matter. Of course, they bungled it. That and other absences of the names of politicians and bureaucrats, such as those in Toronto City Hall, whom the press has reported receiving scads of cash in connection with computer leasing scandals, never seem to be investigated. I've concluded Revcan doesn't do government.

Canada had annexed all the northern territories, and Mr. Claus, residing at the North Pole, had thus become a resident of Canada for tax purposes.

Of course, that sounds bizarre, but does the following real case sound any less so?

Tim Issac is a famous auctioneer and antique dealer in New Brunswick. He was so well known that, when it came time to dispose of the estate of Lady Beaverbrook, Issac got the job. As well as being an auctioneer, he had a high profile in the community because of his political work for the Liberal Party. Starting in 1988, Tim got audited, and it went on for over a decade. What was Revcan looking for? Hidden income? Inflated expenses? Possibly phony tax shelters? No, none of those schemes or any other financial malfeasance — it was looking for a conviction. When the issue went to court (not to Tax Court), the Revcan agent Ms. Nicola Robichaud's primary report, an internal Revcan document, was obtained by the defence. Robichaud wrote in September of 1998 under the heading "Pertinent Case Selection" that "This case is important for a number of reasons: Mr. Issac is a prominent businessman in Saint John. There has not been a prosecution in this community in a number of years. Prosecution of such a prominent businessman would serve as a public reminder that the department will not tolerate tax evasion." Ms. Robichaud went on to defend this statement in court. Here you have a Revcan agent painfully explaining to a judge, as if he were a child, the importance of getting the occasional high-profile conviction. Sort of like having a prostate check once a year. There was no talk of obtaining revenue for the state or whether Mr. Issac had misrepresented his income; if Revcan could find no misstatement, then it would create one if necessary.

I am now going to take you into the cloak-and-dagger operations of Revcan. It completed its 1988 audit in April of 1992 and advised Issac's accountant, James McAllister, that no further payments were necessary and that no changes needed to be made to Issac's accounting methods. That was its position for public consumption, the cover story, but it wasn't finished. On a dark and stormy night in Saint John, New Brunswick, James McAllister was having a drink in a local pub called Sherlock's when a femme fatale approached him. In spite of her disguise (if she had one), he recognized her as Marie Donahue, one of the senior people in the Saint John CRA office. After plying him with liquor and working her wiles on the accountant, she popped the question: what had Revcan missed in its audit of Issac? McAllister, being a professional accountant, advised the Revcan agent that a public bar wasn't the place to be discussing the tax matters of his client. My notes don't indicate if she was taken aback by this statement or what the size of her bar bill was while in pursuit of damning information.

In 1992, not content with having been unsuccessful in finding something in Issac's finances on which to pounce, Revcan did a lifestyle audit. This involves looking at the victim's expenditures versus his income and financial assets. In August of 1999, Revcan accused Issac of evading $41,000 of taxes on unreported income of $160,000. Revcan offered to cut a deal. It had what it wanted, a name to put in the newspaper. Nicola Robichaud admitted in her testimony that Revcan had as an objective the prosecution of seventy-five percent of the referrals and that successful (but not unsuccessful) cases were to be publicized. After all, it had put out the news to the media on four different occasions with an erroneous inflated amount and the information that Issac's wife had been charged — both wrong. When informed by e-mail of its errors, Revcan persisted in reporting the false information. Issac could probably have got off with a fine and some restitution. But as his lawyer said, "You're either a virgin or not, and you're either guilty of fraud or not."

In court, Issac's lawyer destroyed Revcan's lifestyle audit by showing money from the refinancing of real estate properties, the sale of bonds, the cashing of life insurance policies, and nontaxable profits from the sale of their home. All of this and more were reported and explained to the Revcan investigators before the trial. They refused to consider it at that time, obviously because they needed Issac in the dock to be able to use his name, and they had made an investment in him.

So, as recently as 1998, CRA was pursuing people of "high profile" not because these people may have misrepresented their income but because they were in fact successful. Is that legal? Probably not. It certainly violates Revcan's internal guidelines obtained from CRA's own *Tax Operation Manual (TOM)*:

> 1) Every case will be referred to the Department of Justice with a recommendation for criminal prosecution where a full scale investigation has been completed and which can be supported by accumulated evidence of fraud and mens rea indicating guilt beyond a reasonable doubt.

> 2) The case selection will be made within the terms of the best

case concept, of which $15,000 Federal tax should be considered the guideline for any case. Where the case particulars fall outside of these parameters and the Chief of Special Investigations is of the opinion a case should be pursued because of extenuating circumstances (e.g. counseling others to evade tax, previously prosecuted, etc.) the prior approval of the District Office Director should be obtained.

3) No other circumstances should normally be allowed to bear on a decision to prosecute. The recommendations should be based on the facts and evidence and not take into account the position in the community of the taxpayer concerned.

Compare section 3 and the statement of Nicola Robichaud about how Tim Issac was selected. And what about section 1? Was the investigation so complete as to ignore the information regarding the source of funds accounting for the lifestyle? Also, the $15,000 threshold in section 2 should explain to you why, when you see convenience stores where the cash register seldom rings, the situation is allowed to prevail. The cash transactions never see the light of day, nor are they reported to CRA, but the amount of money recoverable is below the threshold. So in the prosecution of tax fraud, the essence isn't to uphold the law but to make a buck.

But the next concern was whether or not Ms. Robichaud was being completely candid or if she might have been directed to Mr. Issac by a higher order. As many of you know, the political parties of Canada want you to vote for their candidates. However, they aren't particularly happy about your choosing the particular candidates, so they like to handle this onerous task for you. The Liberal

Party of Canada in particular has a no-nonsense attitude about choosing candidates. In 1993, the nomination for the Liberals in a Saint John riding was promised to a man named Joe Boyce, who had the support of the local riding association. Tim Issac pledged to be his campaign manager. The Liberal Party had a change of heart and bumped Joe Boyce for Pat Landers (a very good friend of Jean Chrétien's wife). Boyce ran as an independent, which split the Liberal vote and led to the defeat of the Liberal candidate Pat Landers by Elsie Wayne of the Conservatives. When Boyce ran as an independent, Issac, as an honourable man, kept his word and acted as his campaign manager. After Landers lost, Issac was informed by an anonymous phone call that he would be punished for splitting the vote and thus allowing Wayne to win. Five weeks after the warning, Issac was under investigation by CRA. Could this be a coincidence? Maybe, but later I will tell you of another two cases where an audit can be traced back directly to matters other than financial. More coincidences?

The use of the income tax system, and I stress the words *income tax,* to attack enemies of the state or its leaders is not uncommon. Look back to Richard Nixon, who, as president of the United States, would attack his perceived enemies through the income tax system. More recently, Vladimir Putin has used the income tax system to lay low his enemy, who controlled the Yukos Oil Company. In the case of Yukos, an income tax claim was made, and when that was paid another claim was presented, until the company and its owner could no longer withstand the assault of the tax collectors, and Mr. Putin managed to destroy the asset base of his perceived enemy. How can that happen? you may ask. It happens because taxable income is a moving target. In the politicians' eyes, small for my friends and large for my enemies. The corporate welfare ladled out in Western countries is just a form of income tax reduction for friends of the ruling class at the time.

How did the Issac case get resolved? On February 2, 2002,[12] Judge Stymiest of the Provincial Court threw out the charges, citing them as "an abuse of process." The judge was appalled that CRA mixed an investigation with an audit (quite common at the time), that Issac had been investigated or audited on three occasions in one decade, and that the CRA agent Robichaud was willing to admit that the dictates of the *Tax Operation Manual* were ignored. Did Robichaud get disciplined? Did Donahue have to hang up her femme fatale outfit? Will we ever know? Did Tim Issac get punished? Yes, to the tune of $150,000[13] in legal costs. Money likely lost as a result of costing Chrétien's wife's friend a parliamentary seat or being too successful. Issac's name was besmirched as Revcan never publishes its failures or apologizes for declaring a person a tax cheat without a court decision.

How can the average Canadian avoid this kind of horror? My grandmother gave me some good advice as a result of the atrocities committed against the Greeks in 1923 by the Turks. The Treaty of Lausanne ending the war

[12] Note that this nonsense started in 1988! The final case was heard in the New Brunswick Provincial Court, Judicial District of Saint John, in front of Judge Irwin Lambert on April 29, 2002, and the decision was given on May 22, 2002.

[13] The courts' attitudes have changed toward Revcan. Nowadays, when the boys and girls of the tax department act too far beyond the law and cause too much damage, the courts will award damages to the taxpayer. There is a case coming up showing that.

between the Turks and the Greeks called for the exchange of populations. The Greeks in Turkey, some who had lived there since before the birth of Christ, were to be expelled. My Greek grandmother was one of those and had a very good friend whose father was a jeweller. That girl arrived at the disembarkation dock in Smyrna well dressed and wearing some rings. The Turkish guards noticed her and then her rings. They cut off her fingers to get the rings. Now that's what I call direct taxation!

So there is one answer. Don't be visible. But what if you are someone like Céline Dion who needs visibility to succeed? Then, like her, you must be prepared to be abused, and she was, but I digress. To that later.

Issac had to pay the legal costs because Revcan was threatening him with a tax evasion conviction, which carries jail time. If you are being pursued with a conviction in mind, there is little you can do other than flee. However, if you have no assets in Canada, then the *Tax Operation Manual* could come to your aid in that there is less than $15,000 to be recovered, and you can make this known to the investigators, and they should, according to their rules, back off.

The Golden Rule (he who has the gold makes the rules) in all of this is that, if you keep all your assets outside Canada, you are unlikely to attract the attention of Revcan; it will be faced with a collection issue that can never be resolved in its favour. You will become the "client" (as Revcan calls us) that no collection agent wants. Remember — show no rings, and you get to keep your fingers!

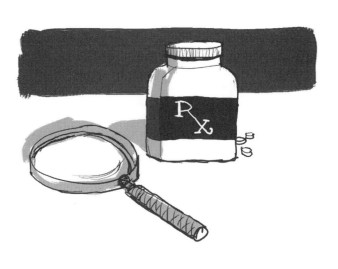

CHAPTER 3

Group THERAPY

HOW REVCAN CHOOSES ITS DANCE VICTIMS

Every year at some secret location in Canada a serious decision will be made affecting possibly thousands of Canadians. None of them will have the faintest idea of how that question was decided, but many will be affected. The tax collector's question of who gets audited is answered at this time. In 1991, pharmacies were chosen — leading to one of Revcan's greatest defeats and embarrassments.

It all started in June of 1991 when John Mark Freeman, an investigator, not an auditor, was examining pharmacies in the Kitchener, Ontario, area. He was sure that some pharmacists were filling prescriptions for cash and not reporting the sales. To his horror, he discovered suspicious payments by generic drug manufacturers in the form of cash and gifts to the pharmacists. They were being made secretly. Oddly, this was the result of a government program.

Prior to 1985, the generic drug manufacturers openly paid a rebate to pharmacists based on the volume of products they sold. This rebate encouraged them to sell generics, and the two big generic firms, Novapharm and Apotex, would clearly indicate to the vendors the amount in rebates they were to receive and on which they would pay income tax. After 1985, the Government of Ontario put an end to the rebate practice when it introduced its "Best Available Price" drug program for impoverished citizens. The problem for Novapharm and Apotex, keen competitors, was that the rebate program was something neither could give up without losing sales. Therefore, the rebates were paid in a more surreptitious manner. Most of the pharmacists declared these earnings, which proved to be a good policy since the manufacturers claimed the payments on their federal corporate tax filings as an expense.[14]

One man, Ronald Cowell, who ran a chain of stores under the name Dial Drugs, decided not to show these payments in his income and had the funds sent to banks, merchants, and service providers in Florida. Clearly a case of tax evasion and punishable. Some $228,104.61 later, Revcan pounced. Cowell didn't serve a day in jail, nor did he have to pay a fine or penalty. What should have been a piece of cake turned out to be pie in the face for Revcan. It all stemmed from arrogance and ineptness.

Freeman, the investigator, couldn't believe his luck. He

[14] However, the Province of Ontario was never notified by the feds that the unacceptable rebate program was continuing since that would have violated the taxpayers' confidentiality. So you had the federal government taxing an illegal activity and not reporting it to the provincial government.

was on to something big, and a flurry of memos went to head office in Ottawa. Freeman and his boss, a Mr. Eberleigh, wanted a national program. But by this time Freeman was hot on the investigative trail (note, not an audit trail) and demanded that the two major generic drug firms cough up their income statements. While doing this, he found out that the firms were under a compliance audit and thus couldn't be part of his investigation since audits and investigations can't be blended. Not to be rebuffed, Freeman went to Novapharm and demanded that its executives "cooperate" with his investigation. The senior management of the firm told him to get lost. Hardly the proper respect to show a hardened Revcan investigator, but there was nothing he could do but slink away in his trench coat and fedora. Novapharm could hide behind its ongoing audit, and Freeman hadn't charged Cowell. Therefore, search warrants wouldn't be forthcoming.

Stymied, Freeman had a brain storm. Why not conduct an audit of Cowell and Dial Drugs? Cowell would provide all his information believing he was being audited, while in fact he was being investigated. Admittedly, the information gained through the audit could not be used for a prosecution, but there was an easy way around that problem. After obtaining the information needed, charge him, get a search warrant, and then claim that the information was obtained during the search. Brilliant? Not quite.

Right from the start, Freeman was wrong footed. He demanded that any documents relating to rebates seen by the auditors looking into Novapharm and Apotex be sent to him. Big mistake. Subsequently, the judge hearing the trial noted that it was already clear that an investigation of Cowell was under way and that to use documents obtained from an audit (even a third-party audit) was illegal. But that was a minor indiscretion compared to what was to come.

Revcan was aware and had informed its special investigators that the criminal aspect of the administration of the Income Tax Act must

> conform to the Charter of Rights and Freedoms; that special investigation staff shouldn't put themselves in a position of directing a compliance audit for the purpose of gathering information for a search warrant; that an investigator is a person in authority whose primary function is to pursue criminal prosecutions of individuals involved in income tax offences; that an auditor, acting as an agent of an investigator, will inherit the same responsibilities as the investigator; and that, in interviewing either the taxpayer or his agent and specifically accountants, an investigator (or an auditor acting on behalf of an investigator) should identify himself as such.

This is very important. Once an auditor knows of an investigation of someone he is auditing, the auditor becomes a de facto investigator. He is no longer an auditor.

The above paraphrases the *Tax Operation Manual*. It is very concise and specific. But Freeman chose to ignore this, as Robichaud had ignored the TOM in the Issac case. To make matters worse, Freeman couldn't have been unaware of the dictates of the TOM since he had previously received a commendation for the preparation of a checklist for compliance auditors when fraud was suspected!

In November of 1993, Freeman met with Art Payne, who had been an investigator for fifteen years but was now auditing the underground economy. Interestingly, Freeman, at Cowell's trial, had no recollection of the meeting, although Payne did. Payne then went on to review the drug company material and met with the RCMP and a Mr. Grundy, who'd been Cowell's/Dial's auditor. Payne went to the accountants for Cowell/Dial and claimed that he was there regarding the sale of seven pharmacies by Dial. This was obviously a bold-faced lie. Payne was still meeting Freeman (meetings during which no notes were taken and memories of which were necessarily vague) and remained under his direction. He was doing an investigation for Freeman. Now, bearing in mind the clause "an auditor, acting as an agent of an investigator, will inherit the same responsibilities," it is obvious that Payne was conducting an investigation on behalf of Freeman while not informing the defendant.

As a result of the work done by Payne, masquerading as an auditor, the bulk of the investigation was completed, and the conclusion was that Cowell was evading income tax. Freeman passed on his information to a Mr. DeLeon, whom the judge in the tax evasion trial of Cowell thought was one of the few credible witnesses put forth by Revcan. Yes, few if any of the government's witnesses, except one, were considered truthful in court.

Realize that at this point in time the information accumulated by Freeman would have been inadmissible in a court since it had been obtained as a result of an audit. To sanitize the information, DeLeon applied for search warrants of Dial's accountant's offices and Cowell's home. To the miraculous surprise of all those involved in the searches, the information they sought was exactly where they looked for it. It was a brilliantly conceived and executed operation. No one mentioned that Revcan had already collated and sorted the information in its own offices prior to the raids. Although DeLeon may have been honest in his testimony, he certainly had no compunction in breaking Revcan's rules. The searches were conducted in November of 1994 under a warrant arising from a criminal investigation of Cowell. Remember that he was being investigated as a criminal. The audit phase was finished and could not be reactivated. DeLeon didn't let this stop him from using a third-party demand *(an audit and compliance tool)* to get Cowell's bank records in March of 1995, after the investigation was under way and audit measures couldn't be used against Cowell. So four months after admitting that the criminal investigation was under way through the undertaking of a search, Revcan illegally used an audit tool from which Cowell had no protection.

By the time Revcan was willing to go to court, it had misrepresented itself (auditor versus investigator), stolen information (records obtained through an audit while actually an investigation), and lied (honestly, it insisted, this really is an audit of your sale of stores, not an investigation). From my reading of the trial transcript, it is possible that perjury was committed by the Revcan witnesses at the subsequent trial.

Why would the Revcan lads be so brazen about violating all the department's internal rules? Because they could. They didn't consider that anyone would have the money or the time to question their actions. They had probably gotten away with similar behaviour previously. They certainly seemed to have a system set up to violate taxpayers' rights and the laws of the land. Regrettably for Freeman, Payne, and DeLeon, their victim, Cowell, went to court.

When the judge heard of the actions of Freeman and

Payne and their failed memories, he was appalled. Revcan pulled out all the stops, even quoting embarrassing Supreme Court cases such as that of *Del Zoto.*[15] Justice Lenz, a man of sterner stuff, was not amused. He didn't even chuckle when he was told that to protect itself the tax department had provided a "sanitized" version of the *Tax Operation Manual* to the defence attorneys rather than the real one. Between his doubts about the veracity of Revcan's witnesses and the complete violation of Cowell's rights, the judge felt that the charges should be stayed and so ordered. The end result was that Cowell got away with tax evasion, but it could and will never be proven. The case[16] cannot be reopened.

Cowell probably ran up a legal bill that would buy a good SUV, although a major portion if not all of it would have been picked up by Dial Drugs as a tax deductible expense. Obviously, the question is how could Cowell have avoided all this? Remember that he first fell into the gaze of Revcan as a result of the audit of pharmacies' cash sales. He was part of a group. He could do nothing about that. If you are part of an element of the economy that does a lot of cash transactions, recognize that Revcan will audit you or members of your profession just to maintain a fear factor. Be squeaky clean. It is a mistake of major proportions to evade tax since doing so is a criminal offence. When you cut through all of the bafflegab, the essence of tax evasion is to lie to Revcan. Although it can lie to you, as it obviously

[15] In this infamous 1999 instance, the lawyers for Revcan successfully argued that their employer could use investigative techniques that violated Mr. Del Zoto's constitutional rights because there was justification in a system of government that depended greatly on tax revenue. The government won the case, allowing the abuse of constitutional rights, but only for taxation.

[16] Information on the trial is filed under Brantford Court file no. 95-3100.

lied to Cowell and his lawyers, you can't lie to it without penalty. As for penalties, I'll bet that, if you call down to the Kitchener, Ontario, CRA office, you'll still find Payne, Freeman, and DeLeon pursuing taxpayers — and probably with more exalted positions.

Okay, let's say that Payne, Freeman, DeLeon, et al. had just fallen off the wagon and as first-time offenders shouldn't face any censure. The whole matter was cleared up with no harm to anyone (except Cowell for his large legal bill). By 2001, though, Revcan learned its lesson not to violate taxpayers' rights by using audits for other than what they are meant to be — an examination (not an investigation) of the taxpayer. Regrettably, the story doesn't terminate with such a happy ending. We fast-forward to March 2001. Yup, the boys were at it again.

Ontario Court Judge Donald MacKenzie refused to lower damages of $230,000 assessed against Revcan and payable to Mr. Linas Saplys. The court had stayed a series of charges against Mr. Saplys in the previous December when it was exposed in court that Revcan was performing illegal acts once again. The judge threw out a series of charges against Saplys because the case was plagued by inordinate delays, an unacceptable lack of disclosure to the defence, and — get this — *improper investigative techniques.* The judge's comment was that, by using its auditing powers to unfairly search for criminal evidence, Revcan had committed a "repugnant act."

If you analyze this carefully, you'll note that this act was committed in Ontario, the same place as the Cowell case, at about the same time. I guess improper use of audits is like the flu. Once it takes hold in one office it jumps to others and infects whole departments. Is there a cure? You bet there is. If Revcan had to pay the court costs and the fines and penalties it was hoping to impose on the taxpayer to that defendant if it lost its case, then there would be much more rigorous abidance by its own rules. Somebody's career should have ended the day Saplys got his cheque. I'm certain that while you read this, Canada's Income Tax Act and its application as defined in the *Tax Operation Manual* are being violated. Somewhere in this great country of ours, there is some Canadian whose rights are being violated. They are being told that they're being "audited," while in fact the audit has nothing to do with tax liability but is an attempt to illegally gain information about third parties or proceed with an investigation by stealth.

Until the cost of the violation of taxpayers by Revcan goes up dramatically, there will be no impetus to stop this abuse. When the costs become excessive, bureaucrats will demand that all audits be justified through an authority that has the right to fire anyone proposing an audit for other than what it was meant. When will that happen? When the judiciary in this country acts like it has in many instances to shape legislation. That action will be to impose financial penalties on Revcan of the maximum allowable.

To quote Howard Morton, a lawyer in the Saplys case, "The real irony is that Revenue Canada expects Canadians to be so honest and straightforward in preparing their tax returns, yet they exhibit that they have absolutely no regard for the rights of taxpayers, for the Charter of Rights or the law of the land."

CHAPTER 4

How Dare YOU!

MY OWN RUMBA WITH REVCAN

So far, we have seen that, if you are high profile or in a target group, you can end up at the wrong end of a Revcan audit. There is another way. Revcan can end up auditing you because it wants information about some third party. Hey, you say that doesn't sound legitimate. Well, actually it's not, but as you have seen the rules are malleable for the toilers in the tax vineyard. I will give you two cases.

The first and obviously most important to me is mine. As you can well imagine after writing two books on tax avoidance, *Take Your Money and Run* and *My Blue Haven,* I was stricken from the Minister of Revenue's Christmas card list. The department was so annoyed at my perceived antisocial behaviour that I was singled out for punishment.

However, the problem facing Revcan was that I no longer lived in Canada. When I left Canada and became a resident of Ireland, I closed off all my connections and paid all my taxes due to the old country (Canada). I was an economic migrant living in the upscale neighbourhood of Dalky, Dublin, with Bono from U2 and the managing director of the Wedgewood company staying nearby. To do so, I had to pay all of my current and future taxes due to Canada. This I did with great glee.

But I forgot about an old income-averaging annuity. It was a structure set up many years ago to alleviate the tax burden on individuals who had spikes in their incomes. People such as entertainers and sports performers, not to mention young stock market bucks, often had single years where their income was higher than that for their average years. I took advantage of that program, which allowed you to set up an income-averaging annuity by which you'd receive an annuity payment that offset the interest on the money you borrowed to buy the annuity. You never received any money since the trust company setting up the annuity made out a cheque for the annuity income to itself to cover the bill for the interest that it charged to itself. As you can imagine, this system was invisible to the annuitant — me. I received no money and paid none out; it all happened at Laurentian Trust. So far, so good.

I was constantly receiving mail from Revcan even though I didn't live in Canada. I was as Irish as Guinness. While I was on holiday in Greece, I received more drivel from the boys and girls, particularly one Barry Lacombe. I wrote back to Barry and told him that I was tired of playing trivial tax pursuit and would answer no more of his inane questions unless he was willing to pay my $300/hour consulting fee. I sent the letter from Greece. Barry then immediately wrote back and announced that Revcan had changed my residency from Ireland to Greece. This changed things considerably. Barry was so interested in my residency because he'd found these annuity payments I was ostensibly receiving. As a resident of Ireland, I could receive them, if I actually received them, tax free because of the Ireland-Canada tax treaty. I had a letter from Revcan saying that I was a resident of Ireland. I sent it to Barry. It didn't matter. As an assistant deputy minister of Revcan, he didn't have to accept the dictates of Revenue Canada. So he made me Greek! His reasoning was that I'd sent him a letter from Greece — therefore I was a Greek resident. My only consolation was that I hadn't sent the letter from Albania or Turkey; being Greek by descent, I would hate to be declared an Albanian or Turkish resident. As a result of having received annuity income (which never touched my palm), I needed to file a tax form, according to Barry. Filing a Canadian tax form is like stepping into a starving lion's cage with a leg of lamb in your teeth. I told Barry I wasn't stupid enough to bare all my financial affairs to Revcan seeing as I didn't live in Canada and my finances were none of Revcan's bloody business. I did explain, however, the circumstances of the annuity payment that offset an equal interest expense. I also explained to Barry that he could find no cheques issued in Canada that had my name on them. Therefore, where did he get the idea that I had received income?

Now, the amount of annuity income was less than my personal deduction, so under no circumstances could there be any tax due, but Barry claimed that withholding tax hadn't been paid on the annuity payments. Whoa! Withholding tax is a tax paid by a payer to a foreigner. So

Laurentian Trust had paid me, a foreigner, but hadn't withheld the tax due, so it had a tax liability. Not in Barry's eyes. The unpaid withholding tax was my responsibility. I tried to explain the concept of withholding tax to Barry — a tax withheld by a payer. He couldn't grasp that. If the withholding tax wasn't withheld, it wasn't my responsibility. That's what the Income Tax Act says. As well, the *Tax Operation Manual* says that, when there is tax payable, the collector pursues the person least able to withstand the department. Seeing as I no longer had any income or assets in Canada, it was obvious that Barry wasn't going to collect from me. So he could, if he wanted to, collect the withholding tax from Laurentian Trust. It operated in Canada and had super-deep pockets. But, alas, Barry wasn't into collecting tax; he was into establishing a tax liability. Ah, yes, another violation of Revcan's rules.

So Barry got a judgment against me in Tax Court. Then someone did a really nasty thing. He or she found the low guy on the collections totem pole and gave him the account. When I read the file that Revcan kept on me (ACSES files of Canadians of interest to Revcan are kept by the department), I was amused. Peter Zevenhuizen starts out full of enthusiasm. He then notes in the file that the client has no driver's licence, no residence, no bank accounts, no brokerage accounts, and no assets. He doesn't even have an OHIP card. You can feel the enthusiasm fading with each new page and revelation. But Peter has all the big guns of Revcan working for him, and one of them gets a hit. There appears in the City of Toronto records the purchase of real estate by a company controlled by someone called Sally Doulis. The tax cowboys swoop on the office of the lawyer for the company buying the property, Minotaur

Capital. They demand that she cough up all the records of Minotaur Capital in her possession. She demurs. So Revcan goes to court and gets an order for the records to be released. But only the financial records. Peter Zevenhuizen and his buddy try to bluff their way into all the records, but by law they can get only the financial records. You may well ask how a Revcan collection agent can get the records of a lawyer's client. What happened to client confidentiality? When it comes to a question of Revcan getting its proverbial pound of flesh, nothing is allowed to get in the way. So much for your lawyer-client confidentiality.[17]

The financial records of my wife's company alone obviously were useless as far as information about me, the object of Peter's mission. Peter knew that there must be something included in all the records. That's why he asked for them in the first instance. So he did a bad thing. He asked for an audit of my wife's company. The nice Mr. Lui from the International Audit of CRA showed up and wanted to chat. My wife said put the questions in writing, and they would be answered. This is extremely important. That nice man standing on your doorstep with his battered briefcase is a financial terrorist dressed to look like Mother Teresa. So remember, nothing by mouth.

It immediately struck me as odd that my wife's Ontario real estate holding company would be audited by International

---

[17] As the result of a recent National Emergency, the threat of terrorism in the United States, your government has set up a financial monitoring agency to track odd flows of funds, and part of that initiative has been to require your lawyer to report any unusual money transfer by you. Lawyers in some provinces have been fighting this, but you might as well accept that your lawyer and accountant work for Revcan. At the time of this writing, the agency was reported as having been singularly unsuccessful at finding terrorist financing. There were some good tax scores, though.

Audit, Barry Lacombe's bunch. I raised this point some-what later with the Minister of Revenue and got an answer that at best can be described as a tango sidestep, a non-answer. Having been rebuffed at the door and complaining bitterly when informed that the company's gross revenues didn't exceed $40,000, Mr. Lui dutifully sent a two-page list of questions, of which one page concerned only Alex Doulis. Wait a minute — you are doing an audit of Mino-taur Capital, and the questions you ask are who controls Liberty Consulting and who are the directors of Liberty? I looked at the envelope. Yup, addressed to Minotaur, but most of the questions were about a foreign company and a nonresident Canadian.

Revcan has an ongoing problem. To facilitate the move-ment of its auditors through the financial jungle, it has made them agents of the crown. That's what a policeman is, an agent of the crown. When someone is sworn in as a Revcan auditor, it makes him an agent of the crown. What happens when a policeman retires or quits? Does the crown de-swear him? Not possible. So the guy remains an agent of the crown. Likewise a Revcan auditor. Although this person may no longer work for Revcan, he can go to its offices and demand records. He has some pretty awe-some powers, like those of a policeman. What can Revcan do when one of its auditors turns against it? It's sort of like Dobermans, they only kill their masters.

I showed Lui's letter to Minotaur (full of third-party questions) to a defrocked Revcan auditor but still an agent of the crown, Wally Dove. Wally, a deeply religious man, had worked for Revcan and risen through the ranks to the point where he could see all the disturbing things his employers were doing. So he quit and went back to being an accountant, but as an agent of the crown, still a Revcan auditor. Wally wrote a scathing letter to Lui indicating that it was a breach of the Income Tax Act to ask questions about third parties in an audit.

There was another problem. Minotaur's bookkeeper was always in fear of Revcan and had constantly made errors in favour of the tax collectors so as to never be accused of under-estimating the taxes payable. In a review of the accounts, these errors were exposed and the overpayment reported to Revcan. However, by this point, the audit had disappeared. Letters to Revcan went unanswered. Even threats from Wally Dove couldn't bring the boys out to play anymore.

The audit had been instigated within two weeks of the visit to Minotaur's lawyer's office by Peter Zevenhuizen. It was obvious that he had instigated the audit and used the International Audit department's auditors. It would have been almost impossible to get an auditor from the domestic companies branch to look at the company since there was no money to be found even if there had been errors. Auditors, like collection agents, are promoted on the basis of how much they bring in. How much can you collect from a company with gross income of $40,000 a year? Remember the old rule of netting $15,000 from an investigation? Revcan probably has the same rule for auditors.

I had the file Revcan kept on me. It's called an ACSES file, and I obtained it through the Freedom of Information Act. When I opened it, I was flabbergasted by the first page, which said in bold letters **"BE AWARE THAT THIS CLIENT HAS ACCESS TO THE MEDIA."** When I questioned the Minister of Revenue about this, she said it was routine to add that sort of thing to a file. Sure. I would have felt more at ease if the announcement at the front of the file said something like "BE AWARE CLIENT STILL WEARS WIDE TIES." Maybe your file has that little disclosure on the front page or something as damning, such as "BE AWARE CLIENT WEARS SOCKS WITH SANDALS." As I read through the file, I found that Peter Zevenhuizen, the collection agent, had read my books about tax avoidance. His review of them showed that he'd missed the clever character development and careful setting. I mean, we're talking about one book that had sold 140,000 copies and another 40,000 copies. I was stunned. I called him on the phone and said that I wanted a meeting. I met him at the Front Street West building of Revcan in Toronto at high noon and handed him a copy of each book (signed first editions). I said that I expected him to read them and that there would be a quiz and that less than a sixty percent score would require rereading. I ruined his lunch.

The incident with the books and Wally Dove's letter were turning things sour by this time. I wrote to the Minister of Revenue and asked who had instigated an audit of a company in which my name appeared more than prominently. Her response was that, seeing as the audit was not of Alex Doulis but of Minotaur Capital, she couldn't release that information. It was a question of taxpayer confidentiality. So I had myself appointed as the agent for all taxation matters on behalf of Minotaur Capital using Revcan's form T 1013. I wrote again to the minister as the tax agent for Minotaur Capital, pointing out that there appeared to be a breach of the Income Tax Act and that, if she wished to uphold the act, she was obliged to provide me with the name of the perpetrator, whom I knew was Peter Zevenhuizen, and that, seeing as I represented Minotaur as its agent, she wouldn't be violating taxpayer confidentiality.

She still wouldn't cough up Peter's name. For loyalty, she gets full marks.

I phoned Peter Zevenhuizen and asked him if he had instigated the audit. Not I, said he. Then I mentioned that I was taping the phone call. He immediately hung up. To this day, he won't take a call from me. Have you ever met a bill collector who won't talk to the deadbeat? I have.

I wasn't getting any satisfaction from the folks in Ottawa about who had instigated the audit of Minotaur. They just wouldn't mention Peter Zevenhuizen's name. Wally Dove once more came to the rescue. He told me about the dread all employees and elected government representatives have of Section 337 of the Criminal Code of Canada: "Section 337. Public Servant refusing to deliver property — Everyone who being or having been employed in the service of Her Majesty in right of Canada or in right of a province, or in the service of a municipality, and entrusted by virtue of that employment with the receipt, custody, management or control of anything, refuses or fails to deliver it to a person who is authorized to demand it and does demand it is guilty of an indictable offence and liable to imprisonment for a term not exceeding fourteen years." That is a very powerful piece of law to have working for you because it includes everyone in government and "anything." I attempted to lay a charge under this section since I had made a "demand" to the minister of national revenue. The justice of the peace had never seen the charge before, looked it up in his law book, and turned pale. His action was not to refuse to file the charge but to insist that this was the jurisdiction of the RCMP and that I should take it to them. They said that they don't do criminal charges and that the JP should know this. The Toronto police likewise: nice charge, but nobody there wanted to become known to Revcan. My only course at this point was to file the charge through a criminal lawyer. However, I realized that the threat I had was more potent than the conviction and imprisonment of some government official.

Subsequently, Revcan, the Minister of National Revenue, and all the ships at sea concluded that I was toxic. Somebody could end up in the slammer if they encouraged me any further. I can't find anybody willing to negotiate a settlement of their claim or even to give a cheque to. Even worse, there was Wally Dove lurking in the wings ready to do the no-tax duet with me. It could get worse. Garry Sorenson, another lapsed Revcan auditor, was out there somewhere and might be brought in to make it a trio of one tax protester and two ex-auditors.

Revcan keeps its finger on the pulse of most of the dollars on the move in Canada, and when I reached ripe old age I was sent pension money from CPP. The amount of the cheques would buy lunch for me and my son at Starfish. So a couple of plates of oysters and a few pints and the pension cheque was consumed. When Revcan heard about my expanding girth as a result of acts of gluttony at Starfish, it acted to protect my health and garnisheed my pension cheque. I was still sent a monthly stipend of fifteen dollars as my portion of the CPP, which I blow on a Monte Cristo cigar. So much for government health programs!

I have considered applying to the government for the Guaranteed Income Supplement and my Old Age Supplement. However, I have concluded that if I do Revcan would collect these government payments to me and put them in the government's coffers, which, with the convoluted accounting, would probably be a contribution to the national surplus. So as it stands, the phony tax debt grows daily, and I could care less.

What should you have learned from this? When the auditor arrives, first ask him to write to you, explaining the purpose of the audit, which he is required to do, and then ask him to put all his questions in writing.

If you know the purpose of the audit, then both you and the auditor can dispose of it quickly. The auditor won't want to leave with no results. The longer he stays on a case, the more he is going to need to justify the time spent, so get it over quickly if possible.

With written questions, it is easier to determine the thrust of the audit. As in the Minotaur case, it was quickly evident that this was not an audit of the company but a subterfuge to obtain information about a third party. If the audit contains questions about a third party, inform the auditor that you cannot and will not answer them, and the audit will probably be shelved.

CHAPTER 5

The Fruitcake IN THE FILE

ACCESSING YOUR ACSES FILE

In the old days, when someone was incarcerated in a jail, the friends of the felon would sneak a file to him hidden in a cake so that he might escape by cutting through the bars. Often the file would be in a fruitcake. Once I found a situation where a file was enclosing enough nuts and lemons to be classed as a fruitcake.

Most government departments keep a file on you. The one kept by Revcan if you have tax outstanding or are naughty is an ACSES file. It is available to you through the Access to Information Act. If you are in any discussions with the tax collectors, they will have opened a file on you, especially if you are behind in your payments. If you want to look at this file, you can make an application through the act by obtaining a form from your local post, taxation, or other government office. The office will send you a letter or phone you to determine what exactly you want and then give you some of what you ask for. I strongly recommend that you obtain this information since it gives you an idea of how Revcan is proceeding and what its plans are.

Once you obtain the file, you should read it and then determine what the omitted or blacked-out bits are all about. They are accompanied by the notations "23," "24(1)," "19(1)," "16(1)(a)," and "16(1)(c)." These are the items that Revcan doesn't want you to see. For example, 23 refers to information that is subject to solicitor-client privilege. Well, seeing that you are the client, then there is nothing here that should be deleted. Moving on to 16(1)(a) and 16(1)(c), the only grounds for use here seem to be that information cannot be revealed to you if it interferes with the enforcement of any *law.* The Revcan folks will carpet bomb your file with 16(1) deletions until it looks like Hiroshima. Bear in mind that they are not enforcing a law. They are enforcing an act, the Income Tax Act. Section 16 of the Access to Information Act is riddled with the words *investigation, criminal acts, weapons,* et cetera, so clearly this section cannot apply to an ACSES file, which is in no way an investigation of a criminal act. Unless maybe it was the commission of a criminal act by an employee of Revcan.

What is annoying to Revcan is if you have asked for your ACSES file and then go to the government's privacy commissioner and plead that the use of Section 16 exemptions from your file is unjustified because there is no criminal activity under way and the section is obviously oriented toward illegal undertakings. If you do this as soon as you receive the file, then Revcan will probably have to cough up the info.

There is a time limit to how soon after you receive the file that you can apply, so read early and complain early.

That is annoying to Revcan. What is terrifying is a subpoena of its records. If Revcan goes to court against you, then you can obtain its records through the courts. These records will be complete. As you have seen in the previous chapters, Revcan likes to keep records even if they are about its breaking of the rules. When that happens, things don't look so good when Revcan arrives in court. I have seen cases where there is an appearance of Revcan backing away from court proceedings so as not to have to reveal its activities.

I obtained my ACSES file in November of 2000. It was the size of a phone book. Now remember that I hadn't resided in Canada since the year 1989. So where did all this information come from? It describes in the first instance Revcan's attempt to build a case to assign a tax liability to me. One bright star in the department raises his doubts that I have ever resided in Ireland notwithstanding that I have a letter from Revcan addressed to me in Villa Vico, Dalky, Dublin, Ireland. In that letter, Revcan declares me a resident of Ireland. After reading the file, I questioned how I couldn't be a resident of Ireland after Revcan had declared me as such, and I received a reply that such declarations on Revcan's part are nonbinding. Okay, then which declarations of Revcan's are binding? Perhaps there is a list somewhere.[18]

---

[18] Can you envision the potential liabilities here for the taxpayer? Revcan says we have a deal; then it says the next day the deal isn't binding on Revcan. I saw just such an event occur when a friend of mine, in negotiating a settlement of taxes outstanding (oh, by the way, Revcan will tell you that it never negotiates), reached an agreement with CRA only to have CRA push him into bankruptcy when it realized it might get a few dollars more by reneging on the deal. As well, if Revcan is in punish mode, as was the case with LeDrew, a deal will get cancelled. More about this later.

As I continued through the file, I found that at the outset everyone was very keen. You could tell by the entries from a variety of people. Their names are shown at the left-hand side of the file followed by their comments. It seems that everyone wants to be associated with the big score. As I progressed through the file, though, I got the picture of a lone stalwart cursed with the file, becoming ever more desperate to find a buck.

Remember, your ACSES file is a tool. Take the time to get hold of it.

CHAPTER 6

Ve Haf Vays
TO MAKE YOU TOCK

DECLINING REVCAN'S "REQUIREMENT FOR INFORMATION"

What happens when Revcan needs information from third parties and there is a reluctance by the third party to supply it? Let me tell you.

I was toiling away in my office writing scurrilous books when my phone rang. The man on the other end, I'll call him Larry to protect the innocent (and his wife hasn't given me permission to use his name), told me he had a problem. Larry was a participant in the wholesale used car business. People would buy a dozen or more cars in one place and auction them off in another, taking the inefficiencies out of the market. This is something, as a past stock market participant, I could appreciate. The problem Larry had was that Revcan had begun an investigation of the wholesale used car business because someone in the chain of participants had been carrying on business from an Indian reserve and not paying GST. To Revcan, this was clearly a case of tax evasion, and anyone associated with these transactions was defrauding Canada.

Revcan was therefore able to freeze the bank accounts of those whom it believed to be involved. If there was no defrauding of Canada, then the accounts would be unblocked, and life would return to normal. However, in the interim, Revcan expected you to cooperate. In reality, there was little fear by the tax guys that you'd been evading tax and were about to skip the country with your ill-gotten gains. What it wanted was a lever to get you to talk. Give it names, dates, amounts; in other words, Revcan was blackmailing you with your own money. Now that's a good trick! If you think about this, it is Napoleonic Law rather than British Common Law in that you are guilty until proven innocent.

Larry's concern was that, if Revcan froze his funds, he'd be unable to meet his commitments and as such would lose his acceptance in the wholesale car business. He came to visit me, and I asked him the amount of money under discussion, and he said it was half a million U.S. dollars sitting in a Canadian bank account. I told him that I would open an account with Barclays Bank in the Turks and Caicos Islands and that he should transfer all his funds to the foreign bank. My recollection of the conversation is as follows.

"What good would that do?" he asked. "The feds will see from the wire transfer documentation that I sent the money to Barclays."

"Yes, but Barclays will not allow Revcan to interfere

with or touch your money. You will be able to carry on business except that your cheques will be drawn on a foreign bank and your deposits will go offshore."

"How can they defy Revcan?" he asked.

"Larry, you are just like every other Canadian in that you believe Revcan is all powerful. It only has power in Canada and that only because the government has passed a number of laws allowing the tax collectors to get around English Common Law, on which our system is based. Under ours and any other legal system based on English Common Law, taxes owing are not a debt. *Black's Law Dictionary* defines debt as an amount of money owing as a result of the provision of a product or service. Revcan has provided you with no service or product; therefore, a debt can't exist. To aid collection, the government has had to jump through some legal hoops. Although they can pass these laws in Canada, they cannot export them. So when a Canadian taxman goes to a foreign jurisdiction seeking a writ based on a collection matter, the foreign civil law will not support his claim — no product or service, no debt — no debt, no collection."[19]

I transferred Larry's funds, and he went on doing business as before. When the Revcan cowboys arrived, they were incensed with Larry for having moved his money out of the country, but to receive his cooperation in their investigation they had to be polite since they had no way to force him to talk. They called him sir a lot.

You may wonder how the Revcan lads and lasses can access Larry's or any other bank account. It is done through

---

[19] Collection is a civil matter, and it is unlikely that Revcan will receive cooperation from any foreign jurisdiction. However, in an evasion situation (a criminal act), some governments will likely assist Revcan.

a "Requirement for Information" (RI). This is a legal document that must be signed by the local tax office supervisor, the senior individual for taxation. It must be delivered by hand or registered mail. The RI must ask for specific information, and the banks are obliged to provide it. However, the banks are not allowed to provide any other information than that demanded. If an RI doesn't answer the questions Revcan was asking, then a new RI has to be sent. Tax guys can't depend on a previous RI and expand its horizons. Bank branches will often respond to a casual request for information from CRA, believing that they have to respond to every request when in fact only a properly constructed RI need be responded to. Your bank isn't obligated to tell you that someone has been snooping around your account unless you send the bank a written request to inform you of any and all inquiries made regarding your account. As well, your bank may try to charge you for the cost of collecting information for the RI. This is not your expense, and you do not have to pay it. But then that raises the question "Why are you banking in Canada?" Once having used an RI to obtain the information it wants regarding the account, Revcan can then freeze the amounts by claiming there is the probability of tax evasion and hence a need to protect what might be the Government of Canada's assets.

Revcan, as you must have concluded by now, is in the information business as much as it is in the money-collecting business. Revcan is your silent partner who has only a tangential knowledge of how you are generating money for it.

Thus, it had to put the squeeze on Larry to expand its knowledge base. I was saddened to hear that four months later Larry had a heart attack and died. I was also berated by his wife for not having made her a signatory on the account, a process that took two months of my time after his death. I believed at the time that his death was partly the result of the strain placed on him by Revcan, but then death by taxation is not uncommon. I will tell you about such an incident later.

You may have concluded that the investigation of Larry's business was not an audit. You are correct. There was an investigation under way, and the audit process couldn't be used. An auditor has broad powers to obtain information more so than an investigator. I don't know whether or not the investigators had sent an RI to Larry's bank to gain information, but they were obviously constrained in how they proceeded, and their only weapon was intimidation. Obviously, the remedy I provided for Larry has applicability to anyone in fear of being intimidated by Revcan. The answer is to bank somewhere else, and it should be in a tax haven.

CHAPTER 7

Death by TAXATION

REVCAN'S AWESOME POWER TO HARASS

One of the worst cases of abuse by Revcan involved the Stephan family. It started in September 1993. Tony Stephan and his wife, Debora, were approached by Revenue Canada for $27,170 in back taxes. He was unable to hire an accountant to verify the charge, so Revcan put it into collection and started pursuing the family. Subsequent records indicate Revcan was aware that the family was in dire straits, with the family home facing foreclosure and the utilities threatening to cut off services. The tax collectors ignored their department's hardship policies, which declare that the collection procedure cannot be so rigorous as to place the taxpayer in a position of destitution. Forcing you out of your home or seizing your tools is proscribed. But still the collectors continued to push the family hard.

Debora committed suicide by asphyxiating herself in her car on January 29, 1994. In her suicide note, she directed that the proceeds of her insurance policy be used to pay the taxman. Ordinarily, life insurance companies are reluctant to pay out in the event of suicide, but in this case her company was more flexible. But not Revcan. Internal documents showed that her death indicated to Revcan that it had the Stephans on the run; it would grant a couple of weeks of truce occasioned by respect for the dead and then fire new salvos.

Tony Stephan tried to lay a charge of breach of public trust with the Lethbridge crown prosecutor against the two tax agents who'd hounded his wife to death. The same day that charges were lodged against the agents, the Stephans' adopted daughter, Linda, and her new company were hit with reports from Revenue Canada that they were to be audited. Revcan wanted tax records going back three years, even though the company had been in existence for only six months and had yet to file a tax return. Revcan wanted to audit tax returns that didn't exist. When Linda called the Edmonton tax office, it claimed to know nothing of the audit.

Allow me to digress for a minute. From this, you can ascertain that, at the first feeling of inconvenience or displeasure by the Revcan horde, the audit demand will be made. It doesn't matter that you are a Canada Pension Plan pensioner on fixed income with no other sources. Our boys and girls at Revcan know you will be upset and inconvenienced. Serves you right for parking in a Revcan reserved space or elbowing your way onto an elevator at the tax office. In some cases after the audit form has gone out and the taxpayer's first response is received, the audit disappears. No mention of it ending — just silence at the other end.

How could it be that the Edmonton tax office knew nothing of the audit? Quite easy, actually. The various departments in Revcan have groups of their own auditors. Sort of like a departmental car pool. So if you wrinkle your nose at an International Audit guy, you could have one of that department's auditors auditing your domestic company. The corporate taxation people in your area probably wouldn't know for weeks that you are being audited. So in the Stephan case, somebody didn't like the idea of criminal charges being laid against tax collectors and immediately called out his auditors without informing the local guys.

You may think it bizarre that Revcan has all these human resources floating around, but it gets worse. While they are undertaking a collection from the Stephans, what would lead someone from Revcan to call Debora Stephan's cousin and ask about the Stephans' marriage? Does that lead to the collection of money? Is the marriage an asset Revcan thought of seizing? The same legions of collection agents have amazing powers. There is none of your financial matters that they can't access, and it seems that even your personal matters are open to inspection.

Don't you wish you could harass the tax guys the way they harass citizens? Well, someone actually did, although it wasn't fatal for the tax collectors.

In early 2000, Scott Manson of Calgary created a $20 million debt from two Calgary tax collectors, Robert McMeekin and David Samson. He then followed this up with liens on their homes and placed liens at the Personal Property Registry in Alberta, thus tying up all their assets. The agents complained to the local police, who laid a charge of harassment against Manson. When the issue went to court, the police officer laying the charge claimed that the creation of a debt was illegal. She was unaware that this is exactly what Revcan does.[20] When questioned why she had concluded the debt was illegal, either through research or consultation, she replied that she'd just felt it was illegal. The harassment charge was thrown out.

Why, you might ask, would someone do this? Manson was more than a little peeved as a result of the tax guys recruiting the help of a local drug dealer and the provincial police to build a case for property seizure and prosecution. They drained his RRSP and during the process confiscated funds for the medicine necessary to keep his father alive. The man died — Scott became annoyed.

---

[20] As noted above, *Black's Law Dictionary* defines a debt as money owing as a result of the provision of a product or service. Gambling debts and taxes don't fall into this definition, so Revcan has created the item known as a "tax debt" and, like gambling debts, has had to find special ways of collection.

CHAPTER 8

Nothing by MOUTH

MAKE THEM PUT IT IN WRITING

The arrival of a Revcan auditor at your doorstep is never going to be a pleasant occurrence. You can make the experience less painful if you realize the following.

1. He can review only this year's and the past three years' filings.
2. There is no information he cannot obtain.
3. All the information he obtains is confidential up to a point.

The auditors can demand information from third parties regarding your finances, and there are any number of devices available for them to obtain information. However, they can't make enquiries about the actions of third parties as a result of auditing you.

When the auditor arrives, provide no information verbally, and don't discuss your financial affairs. Ask, politely, that all questions be submitted in writing. As well, before answering questions, take the auditor's card and write him a letter asking why the audit has been instigated and which specific areas of your finances have attracted his attention. You can demand to know the purpose of the audit. This question should be framed in the context of trying to aid the auditor in his examination. If you can discover what Revcan is looking for and provide answers, the auditor might well disappear. Remember that, the longer the auditor is on your case, the more he has to take in by way of a reassessment. Someone has to pay for his time, and that someone is you. If the auditor walks away empty-handed, there is the implication that the case selection process was flawed. This doesn't look good on some Revcan employee's job evaluation.

Always keep in mind that this is an examination of your affairs. It is not an investigation. If at any time you believe that rather than looking for a reassessment the tax boys or girls are looking for a conviction, confront the auditor with the question *"Am I being investigated?"* The telltale sign is the introduction of new people into the process. If the auditor says that there is a new person taking over or he has a new assistant, then there is probably something more than an audit under way. At this point, some self-review should be undertaken.

1. Can Revcan in any way find an amount of money to dispute that would bring in $15,000 in taxes? That would mean disputed income of around $45,000 assuming a thirty percent tax rate.

2. Can you be considered high profile? Are you well known in your community?
3. Have you annoyed someone in government?
4. Do you have any enemies?

I have heard of occasions of people being reported to Revcan as having undisclosed income simply out of malice. Remember how kids you knew in school would send the local meanie unordered pizza or make stupid phone calls to him? This is the adult version of the same maliciousness.

At this juncture, you have to consider your situation, and you may confirm that this is indeed just an audit. Wait for the auditor's reply to your question about why the examination was undertaken. When you have that reply and the letter with his questions, it's time to get to work. Look at the questions. First determine if any don't concern you, and if there are there will be a theme. It will be about either an institution or an individual. Here are some typical questions.

1. Do you bank with the Wonder Bank of Tax Haven, British West Indies?
2. Who introduced you to Wonder Bank?
3. Does this person bank at Wonder Bank?

The questions can address any number of facets of your relationship with an institution, but you'll quickly determine that the questions are more about the institution than about you.

The questions may be about an individual.

1. What is the business relationship between you and Garth Evader?

2. Where was your business with Mr. Evader conducted?

3. How was payment made by you to Mr. Evader?

4. Does Mr. Evader issue receipts?

It is a violation of Section 231.2(2) of the Income Tax Act to attempt to extract information regarding third parties who are not the subject of the audit. What the above questions have in common is that the answers you provide will in no way assist an auditor to determine the amount of your taxable income. These questions are about third parties. You should inform your auditor that these activities don't comply with the Income Tax Act. You shouldn't respond to any questions that do not refer to your income and expenses as reported on your tax form. Remember that the auditor is there to confirm that the information you provided to Revcan is complete and correct. By "correct" is meant that you may have made an error, but the error wasn't part of an attempt to deceive Revenue Canada. By answering questions about a third party, you are in no way working toward getting rid of the auditor, and you may be implicating yourself. By confronting the auditor, and particularly if you have his questions in writing, he will have to reconsider his position. Knowing that you know he's in violation of the act, he may choose to walk away.

At some point, you may need to contact a lawyer. There are two things to remember about your lawyer. He is bound to report to Revcan any indications of strange money movements. I suspect that many Greeks who throw coins onto dance floors at weddings or hide coins in the New Year's bread could find themselves under investigation since there is no record of how that money changed hands. The same applies to your accountant. The other issue is that your lawyer learned all his law in school. He knows how the law is applied but little about its legitimacy. This is particularly true of Revcan's rules. Revcan auditors whom I have spoken to have shown me that the need to file an annual return depends very much on your circumstances or that the penalties applied in many cases have no legal substance. But more about that later.

CHAPTER 9

Four Wrongs Do
MAKE A RIGHT

•••••••••••••••••••••••••••••••••

THE JUDGES RIDE TO THE TAXPAYER'S RESCUE

If the boys and girls in the tax office go too far, the taxpayer can apply to the courts to have the pursuit ended. This arises when the prosecution in the case has taken steps that put the administration of justice in disrepute. Such a case involved Brian Donovan of New Brunswick.[21] He ran a garage, and there was a discrepancy between what he reported as income and what he appeared to be receiving. The interesting aspect of this case was that Donovan appears to have evaded income tax on $50,000 and gotten away with it.

The avenue for escape for Mr. Donovan was that

[21] See Donovan v. Canada A-671-98.

Revcan had committed four "wrongs" in its pursuit of him. It had committed a "flagrant and egregious violation" of his rights, according to the New Brunswick Appeal Court judges. This case was heard as an appeal because the Tax Court of Canada had ruled against Donovan. As I mentioned earlier, the Tax Court most often rules in favour of Revcan, so that in many instances when either the amount or the outcome is serious the defendant will appeal to the provincial appeal court. In this case, Donovan could have been facing jail time for tax evasion if Revcan had decided to go down that route. However, it seems that the tax collectors realized there was some sloppy work in their pursuit of Donovan, so they decided to pursue reassessment rather than evasion, although that remained a viable possibility. In other words, Revcan launched a civil rather than a criminal action. Perhaps its thinking was that the case was tainted, so it was better to get something out of it than abandon the investment, and a civil action that might not be disputed would be the most cost-effective route.

The first wrong: an auditor went to Donovan's accountant about the numbers, and the accountant showed the auditor a signed draft of the tax filing being considered. The auditor took that and filed it as the taxpayer's annual filing without the taxpayer's knowledge or consent. Can you picture Revcan auditors roaming the country asking for signed but partially completed tax forms for them to file? We would all be in the clink. Speaking of the clink, as you should know by now, it is an offence to file a false tax form or one that you know is likely to misrepresent your income. Hmm, here we have a government tax auditor filing a form that he has every reason to believe is incomplete and later goes on to dispute. Hmm, seems to me that the auditor has counselled and been party to the commission of an illegal act. No, he was not charged.

The second wrong: you guessed it. The auditor, a Mr. MacDonald, decided to take a case-hardened member of the Special Investigations Unit to attend the audit over a period of two days. Neither Donovan nor his accountant was aware that the steely faced individual was not an auditor but LeBlanc, the investigator. Revcan said there was really, honestly, no criminal investigation going on at the time. MacDonald had brought LeBlanc along to "eyeball" Donovan when confronted with the funds' discrepancy. Would the wily investigator see a reaction invisible to the untrained eye? The Appeal Court judges could hardly believe what they were hearing.

This occurred in 1989, ten years before Saplys and Cowell, the two cases where the courts severely slapped the hands of Revcan for having investigators posing as auditors. There appears to be a Chinese wall between the various offices of Revcan in that, when a naughty deed is committed in a jurisdiction, the news that it is frowned upon by the courts doesn't seem to travel very far if at all. As you have read previously, as soon as the SIU investigator appears on the scene, the audit is assumed to have changed into an investigation, and even the auditor is considered an investigator and no longer an auditor. It all seems so incredibly simple and straightforward. If an auditor doesn't want to be part of an investigation, then don't discuss the information with an investigator. So far, we have two wrongs and just two more to go.

The third wrong: after having LeBlanc, the investigator, "eyeball" Donovan, the tax collectors decided to go for weapons of mass destruction. To collect the information they needed for reassessment, they obtained a search warrant. The only problem was that the search warrant they used was unconstitutional. Donovan's lawyer had it overturned and demanded that he, the lawyer, have all the documents seized returned to him. The judge agreed and instructed Revcan to return all the papers to Donovan's lawyer. This only made Revcan's position worse in that, upon return to the lawyer, the material now became privileged. It would be protected by solicitor-client confidentiality. Even worse, the defendant's lawyer would now have all the evidence upon which Revcan had expected to build its case and a good knowledge of what its course of action would entail.

As a long-distance sailor, I can tell you that when things go wrong on a boat they seldom occur as single events. They cascade or occur together. In Revcan's situation with Donovan, I see a man in a leaky boat trying to patch holes while the electrical system is starting to burn from over-exertion of the bilge pump. For Revcan, it led to the most bizarre of the wrongs, the fourth one.

The fourth wrong: the response to the court's demand that the documents be returned to Donovan's lawyer was to try to short-circuit the system. The Revcan lawyers went to a judge and obtained a new search warrant (remember they still have the documents) and didn't bother to inform the judge issuing the new constitutionally compliant warrant that they had the material and had been denied warrants concerning these documents in previous applications. Now armed with a search warrant for material in their possession, they proceeded to Donovan's previous place of business, a now deserted garage, knowing it would be deserted. Yes, I know you are asking, how can someone have a search warrant to find something he already has in his possession? After furiously knocking on the door of the empty building and probably yelling "Anybody home?" they placed the documents on the stoop. They then reached into their pockets and came up with the new warrant entitling them to search the empty garage for financial documents concerning Donovan's business. They didn't have to look far as the documents were right there on the doorstep.

The judge hearing the appeal described the actions of Revcan as "reprehensible as well as illegal." This particular action really got up the nose of the judge because lies had been told to obtain search warrants (perjury) and, by not returning the material to Donovan's lawyer, there was an act of contempt of court. However, nobody in the Revcan ranks was prosecuted; the case was merely thrown out.

What does this case illustrate? First, when Revcan starts an audit, it is difficult to cascade into an investigation because much of the material that could give rise to the investigation has been obtained without the individual's Charter protections. This really puts Revcan in a difficult position because the audit may have shown criminal abuse of the tax system, but that fact is inadmissible because of how it was obtained.

Second, you have the dog-on-a-bone syndrome. If the people working on Donovan's case had just backed off and stuck with a reassessment instead of considering a criminal action, all would have been fine. Once having realized, as they should have, that their efforts were tainted, they should have thrown in the towel. But that would have meant many hours of wasted time without benefit to Revcan that were sure to make their way into annual work performance evaluations of the people involved. Faced with that, and the possibility that because of the small amounts involved Donovan might capitulate, it was a calculated risk. However, Donovan was probably writing off the legal expenses against his garage business, so the choice to continue was obviously, in hindsight, a bad one.

The conclusions are that you should, as previously advised, determine at the outset of an encounter with Revcan whether you are dealing with an auditor or an investigator. Keep good written records of all information provided to an auditor to prevent it from being introduced in an investigation. As well, be aware of the dog-on-the-bone syndrome. The longer the auditor is there, the more desperate he will be for a reward, and the larger it will become. If you can answer his questions and get rid of him, then the sooner he will move on to the dentist next door.

CHAPTER 10

Standing Up TO BULLIES

••

BEFUDDLING THE "INTERNAL COLLECTOR"

Like Dick Turpin, the famous but not too bright English highwayman of the carriage era in England who, after a pint too many, would yell, "All right, I'm going to rape all the men and rob all the women," sometimes actions and the objects of those actions get a little confused in the minds of Revcan's collection agents.

If the audit goes badly, then Revcan will demand that you pay what it believes is the amount outstanding. If you refuse, Revcan will turn the matter over to an internal collection agent, who has some pretty awesome powers. The agent will look at your bank accounts, investment accounts, real estate holdings, and motor vehicle records. As well, the corporate records of the various Canadian stock exchanges are available to him. The bank accounts will be drained and any securities and stock options seized. Although any investment real estate is at risk, Revcan cannot seize your principal residence. It can, though, place a lien on your house so that if you sell it you'll have to pay the lien before you can close the sale. As well, the collection agent is forbidden from taking your tools. This means anything you use to provide your livelihood, including your vehicle. Also, the agent cannot garnishee your income to the extent that you are forced into undue hardship.

The major problem for the collection agent occurs when the assets you use are in the name of someone else, usually a spouse. The collection agent will get a court order to pursue your assets. If the assets were in the hands of someone else two years prior to the court order, then there is no way that the collector can take them. If the transfer occurred within the two years of the judgment, he will claim "fraudulent conversion" and try to overturn the action.

What about joint bank accounts? If Revcan sends an RTP ("Requirement to Pay") to your bank and it refers to a joint account, then the RTP will be returned unexercised. It was common practice for a while in the United States for the IRS to take a cash advance on tax debtors' credit cards as part of the collection process. This has been challenged, however, in the courts (I didn't authorize the withdrawal, nor does the bank have my signature on any documentation — this debt is the bank's!).[22]

What does become tricky is when you show up at your bank with a cheque made payable to you. A cheque is a

---

[22] See "The Power to Destroy," by Senator Roth and William Nixon, for a scary treatise on income taxation run amuck in the United States.

written instruction to a bank from an account holder to pay a certain amount of money to an individual. Your bank will take that instruction and send it to the payer's account to see if it is valid, and if so the amount will be paid to your account. However, Revcan can interfere with this process by instructing your bank to deliver the funds to its own account. By law, the clerk at the counter cannot tell you, if you don't already know, that any cheques you attempt to deposit will be seized by Revcan and that your bank account has been drained. If you don't want Revcan to have the money, what can you do?

You can't take the cheque to just any branch and demand that it honour it. Banks in Canada will not cash a cheque for a non-account holder unless it is a government cheque. However, if you show up at the bank at which the cheque was drawn with a piece of photo identification and just for insurance two other pieces of ID, the bank is required to obey its depositor's instructions. Remember that the clerk is not knowledgeable about the Bank Act and may balk, but the branch manager should know the rules; if not, have him or her call head office.

While you are being pursued, you'll probably be doing much of your commercial activities with cash. If you want to send a small amount (less than a few thousand dollars) to someone, you can always buy a bank cheque or draft at some branch or other. Large amounts are hard to purchase. The bank will ask that you deposit the money in an account and then have the account rather than you personally buy the cheque. This has been instituted to help Revcan impede the flow of untraceable money to those nasty offshore accounts. Another alternative is to go to the post office and buy a postal money order. However, it may cause problems if mailed to someone outside Canada. But then this raises the question I asked before: why are you banking in Canada?

The collector will try to garnishee payments you may receive as salary, pension, whatever. Garnishees as exercised by Revcan will usually not stand up in court. If the issue of hardship is raised in a court, a judge will have to decide if either party would be harmed by staying the garnishee order. If neither party would be harmed, then the garnishee is put aside.

CHAPTER 11

We've Got A SECRET

··

FLUSHING REVCAN ONTO THE DANCE FLOOR

Revcan's stated belief is that the taxpayer's records are confidential. They have to be; otherwise, how can Revcan ensure that the gun runners, dope dealers, and swindlers of this country pay their taxes? Think back to the Cowell/ Dial Drugs case. The Government of Ontario told the drug manufacturers to stop paying kickbacks. So as not to jeopardize their business, the companies continued to pay these kickbacks but did it surreptitiously. Nobody but Revcan knew that the process was continuing. If asked by the province, Revcan would refuse to answer if the kickbacks were continuing, thus ensuring taxpayer confidentiality.

I have had personal experience with taxpayer confidentiality at two levels. In one case, a criminal was allowed to continue his misdeeds; in other cases, taxpayers themselves were protected from using their own information. As well, there are documented cases of confidentiality being compromised. But let's look at the cases I observed.

The first case arose out of a party I attended at my son's loft. There were people from every walk of life, including a number of bike couriers since my son is a devoted cyclist. One of the couriers approached me and asked if it was true that I took people's funds offshore. I replied that I did, but I never discussed these matters outside my office. So we met at my office, and the conversation went along these lines.

"How much cash are we talking about?" I asked.

"About $150,000, give or take."

"And where is it now?"

"Let's say under my mattress."

"Am I to believe," I said, "that you expect me to accept that a bicycle courier could legally amass that much money?"

"That's the catch. Sometimes when you courier certain things you get paid more than for other things."

"I gather that you've been delivering recreational pharmaceuticals."

"Yes, but only hash and pot."

"I admire your sense of morality," I said. "However, the problem confronting me is that this money was accumulated through what would be viewed as a criminal enterprise, and if I touched it I would be accused of money laundering."

"What can I do?" he asked. "I am terrified that I'll get broken into or be home-invaded and the entire stash stolen."

By "stash," I concluded he was referring to the money, not to what in my youth was regarded as the weekend's recreation.

"I am going to give you a toll-free number," I said, "which, just for safety's sake, you should call from a public phone. You will be in touch with Revcan, and they will negotiate a deal with you that will require you to pay some income tax on the money, after which you can deposit it in a bank, and I would suggest a foreign one so that the amount doesn't attract the police."

"Yeah, well, what if the tax guys tell the police?"

"They can't because of taxpayer confidentiality," I said. "If that doesn't work, come back to me, and I'll put you in touch with some people I know who run a bakery in the north end of town. Either way it's going to cost you about thirty-five percent to cleanse the money."

I didn't hear back from my courier friend, but I do see him whizzing around town on his courier runs in the financial district. He always has a big smile for me, so I gather that his problem was solved, and I suspect, because he didn't come back to me, that it was Revcan that laundered his funds. You may believe that criminal activity and taxpayer confidentiality are a limited occurrence and that my experience was exceptional. Not really.

The second instance of a bizarre application of the confidentiality rules involved a client of mine. It is quite acceptable to ask someone if he is no longer beating his spouse. However, even among the most impolite in our society, you wouldn't ask the indiscreet question if you had knowledge of someone else beating someone's spouse. On occasion, Revcan needs information, and the only way to get it is to ask third parties. This is particularly true for the offshore havens. If someone has set up a tax avoidance scheme using a tax haven, then there is no way that anyone in one of those places is going to answer Revcan's questions, and the tax collectors have no way to apply pressure. Obviously, for the tax collectors, the answer is to ask questions where they do have some power, and that is in Canada. A client of mine had some passing knowledge of a slick tax avoidance format using the offshore, and his information was of interest to Revcan. But Revcan couldn't just drop by for a coffee and ask him, so it audited him.

My acquaintance refused to answer any verbal questions and insisted that everything be put in writing. Those questions that pertained to him he dutifully answered. The others he refused to answer. This incensed the tax guys, so they said they wanted to come and interview him. Being a television producer, this man spotted a potential blockbuster video on what a tax audit is about, how it progresses, and what the final outcome is. When he told me about it, I thought it was brilliant. Wouldn't you buy a video on a tax audit if you were a small business owner? As well, the purchase would probably be tax deductible. So as the audit progressed, he scripted it, and when Revcan announced that it would like to interview him he asked for enough time to prepare for the filming of the interview and the visit to his place of business. Below is the verbatim response letter from Revcan.

> From: Tax Avoidance
> S.J. Walker, CMA.
> August 26, 2003.
> Dear Sir/Madam:
> <u>Re: 2001 and 2002 T1 Income Tax Returns</u>
> Further to the comments made in your letter of June 26, 2003 we wish to make the following statement:
> The Canada Revenue Agency does not allow the use of

video or audio recording devices during meetings in order that the confidentiality provisions of the Privacy Act and the Income Tax Act are complied with.

Further to your letter of May 18, 2003 and our letter of June 12, 2003 with respect to your request to have a third party attend a meeting, we must, at this time deny your request. The presence of this "third party professional" would not be for the purpose of being your representative for income tax matters, but for the purpose of publishing an article in a magazine or publication.

In your letter of July 10, 2003, you have requested that we submit our questions to you in writing. A list of questions is enclosed. The written responses to these questions should be submitted to our office within thirty (30) days.

Yours truly,

Let's go through that letter. Paragraph two: "The Canada Revenue . . ." states that CRA does not want recording devices at meetings. What about the client, suppose he does? Whose information is being recorded — CRA's or the client's? If the client is supplying the information, hasn't he the right to keep records of what he is supplying? Can he not keep copies of letters? Can he not, as I have done, publish a copy of correspondence from CRA if the client gives me his permission?

Paragraph three, last sentence: ". . . for the purpose of publishing an . . . publication." I found it difficult to understand what is meant by publishing a publication. I assume that when you publish the end result is a publication. So what if the client wants to throw all of his tax information into the public record? It's being done every day by CRA without the client's consent. Why all the concern? Remember what was at the front of my ACSES file: "**BE AWARE THAT THIS CLIENT HAS ACCESS TO THE MEDIA.**" We know from the *Tax Operation Manual* as quoted in the Issac case that CRA is seeking information to publish when it comes to investigations in which it has triumphed. So one has to assume that publishing is a one-way street for Revcan.

What does Revcan have to fear? You'd think that the auditors' jobs would be easier having a record of all that transpired. At last report, this audit had ground to a halt since neither side was willing to budge.

I'll bet from the above material you have concluded that the protection of taxpayer information is paramount out there in Ottawa. Well, then, what do you make of this?

Toronto Sun, Friday December 10, 1999.

Montreal (CP)

Seventeen restaurants, part of the Nickels chain founded by Céline Dion and her husband René Angelil, were closed Wednesday while Revenue Quebec officials executed search warrants.

A total of 26 warrants on 24 different Nickels restaurants were carried out. The chain's headquarters was also hit. The individual restaurants are operated as franchises, which pay royalties to Dion, Angelil, who doubles as the singer's manager, and another investor.

Managers in several of the restaurants refused comments on why they were being investigated.

Last March and June, seven Nickels outlets were investigated for tax evasion.

The raids were conducted into allegations that three restaurants used illegal "zappers" software programs to make cash sales disappear from their electronic cash registers.

The zapper programs, which cost about $500, are easy to obtain on the black market. They help restaurant owners to under-report revenues and thus evade taxes.

This story was taken from the Canadian Press (CP) news wire and carried in the *Toronto Sun*. Where did the story originate? Obviously with the Quebec tax authorities (about the same time as tax forms start arriving in the mail). Who is being investigated? Certainly not Dion and Angelil. And what about that third mysterious investor? Why aren't we given his or her name? Because it wouldn't have any impact on the reader. If anything, these three people are injured parties as a result of the understating of revenues by their franchisees and hence royalties paid to them.

Was the law broken here? It sure was. The Income Tax Act (subsection 244[1]) requires that charges be laid before a taxpayer's name be made public. Therefore, because Dion and Angelil weren't charged, their names shouldn't have been associated with this matter. To release information about them and their tax matters is a breach of the Income Tax Act (subsection 241).

Suppose Revcan decided to look into the affairs of Lord Black and Hollinger Inc. Can you accept that as well as illegally mentioning the investigation Revcan goes on to list all the shareholders of Hollinger?

You and I both know that if you take the Dion name out of the story there is little to catch the eye. The final absurdity is that Revcan has informed you that, if you are operating a restaurant in Canada with an electronic cash register, there is a way to overcome its record keeping, and that is with a "zapper." You'll also note that you shouldn't pay more than $500 for it and that it is readily available. Regrettably, the 800 number of the distributor of the zapper wasn't provided.

The Dion and Angelil names appeared in the article because they are known to many if not most Canadians. How can these people possibly keep their names out of the paper? Their success depends on having media exposure, but I wonder what kind of impact this exposure had for them. Is there any way they could have avoided the negative information with which they were associated for Revcan's benefit? Not that I can see. If they turn down every business opportunity that comes along and keep their wealth in Canada Savings Bonds, they will be safe. To deprive them of potential business profits is a form of tyranny.

You might conclude that this is an isolated event and only likely to happen to those high-profile Canadians whom Revcan is so keen to publicize in the land of the maple leaf. Well, then, what about Sarah Gernhart?

CHAPTER 12

Pimping for HEALTH CARE

REVCAN'S EMBRACE OF THE CRIMINAL CLASSES

This woman was not the famous actress of similar name. She was not a high-profile Canadian, and, no, the tax department didn't blab her confidential financial information to all and sundry. However, it didn't act to prevent it from being circulated. Ms. Gernhart was involved in a messy divorce, and questions were being raised about which spouse had the ability to provide financial support. The easiest way to determine that was to review the tax-payer's records. This is very difficult to do. Remember the old confidentiality concerns. Well, then, you might ask, how did Ms. Gernhart's lawyers manage to show up in court with her most secret and confidential records? They went to the courthouse and had her records copied for forty cents a page. Her records were at the courthouse because she had challenged her 1994 tax assessment and gone to court to fight it. As a result, her tax records became part of the court record and open to all and sundry. Ms. Gernhart was more than a little annoyed and took the government to court.[23]

A very important conclusion from Ms. Gernhart's case is that, if you are going to have your tax matters adjudicated in court, you should ask for the hearing to be held in camera and to be sealed and not available to the general public. On the other hand, if you have an ex-spouse, business partner, or client whose financial matters interest you, then head off to the courthouse and see if he or she has had occasion to dispute tax matters in court.

There is a propensity for the courts to override the wishes of the defendant for privacy in a case where an important issue has been adjudicated. Such a case concerned Mrs. MacDonald and the payment of bribes.

If you were running a brothel, you'd attempt to keep your business as discreet as possible because, as you'd probably know, living off the avails of prostitution or keeping a bawdy house is a crime in Canada. However, as long as you pay your taxes and bribe the police, it's quite all right.

Brothel owners paying tax and being shielded from the police? Yes, in Canada it is a crime to live off the avails of prostitution, but Mrs. MacDonald did so for a number of years in Vancouver in the 1950s. The problem was she did so in a rather high-class area of the city, and her neighbours, walking their poodles down the tree-shaded streets

[23] See Federal Court of Canada, Docket A-50-97, *Sandra Gernhart v. Her Majesty the Queen.*

of their privileged enclave, became weary of the sight of ladies in stiletto heels. Calls to the police and city hall went unheeded. Could there have been a connection? Were these calls being made to Mrs. MacDonald's clientele?

The brain trust of the area was sure that Mrs. Mac-Donald couldn't possibly have corrupted the higher plane of Canadian government, the feds, so some genius reported her as a tax cheat. Surely a woman running an illegal business wouldn't be so brazen as to report her income to the federal government? Well, yes, actually. The auditors, once alerted, had to proceed, but there is no Revcan auditor who will leave without a bone. Having gone over her books, the auditor would be found remiss if he came back without something. In this case, it was $2,400 worth of liquor that Mrs. MacDonald gave to various members of the Vancouver police force at Christmas (remember this was the 1950s, so that was a substantial amount of booze). The madam had been charging the liquor as a business expense. The auditor claimed it was a gift freely given. They went to court, and the judge ruled that Mrs. MacDonald was running an illegal business and that the payments of bribes were necessary to sustain it and that both Mrs. MacDonald and the Government of Canada would be impoverished if she did not continue to give out liquor to the police. The case still stands in the books as a defining judgment on the issue of bribes and their tax deductibility. Had it not gone to court, we would never have known about it.

So you think it is kind of weird that the Government of Canada would indirectly live off the avails of prostitution. Sort of like pimping. But now you know how your health care costs are paid. Well, the U.S. government went one better. It actually ran a house of ill repute.

In Nevada, prostitution is legal. In 1954, a man with the unlikely name, for his line of business, Bob Confort, founded the Mustang Ranch. It was licensed by the State of Nevada in 1971. Now, because of its nature, the brothel business is a cash business. No one wants to have his credit card bills showing the Chicken Ranch or the Mustang Ranch as having had the benefits of his custom. In 1981, the Internal Revenue Service of the United States decided that Bob was too comfortable. It began an audit of his affairs, and he quickly fled the country. The government had no recourse but to seize his assets, which of course consisted of one of the world's great cat houses. Rather than close it down, the tax collectors realized that their best avenue of recapture of unpaid taxes would be to sell it as a going concern. The General Services Administration of the U.S. government took over a whorehouse.

Word quickly spread throughout Nevada that there was a way to screw the government. Questions were asked about whether the employees of the Mustang Ranch would be classed as civil servants. The story of the Mustang Ranch became public because the U.S. government auctions off the property of tax debtors, and the ranch appeared in the list of assets being sold.

CHAPTER 13

This Is an Emergency!
IS THERE A SENATOR
IN THE HOUSE?

POLITICIANS CAN'T RESIST BENDING TAX RULES

Senator! Senator! This is an emergency! Is there a senator in the house?

How confidential is confidential? What we have seen so far is that taxpayer confidentiality is sort of adhered to. If it is to the government's benefit, the material in your tax file will be deemed so secret that even you will have trouble recording it. On the other hand, if it suits the government and you are rich or famous, the government might be very cavalier with your information. Is there a case where the government endeavoured to protect the confidentiality of a rich and famous taxpayer? Yes.

Take, for example, the Bronfman family. Awesome wealth was created by Sam Bronfman of Seagram's when he competed with Harry Hatch of Gooderhams for the title of biggest bootlegger in Canada during the U.S. era of prohibition. The difficulty that Sam's heirs were confronted with was that all their wealth had accumulated in Canada and attracted the higher tax rates that applied in this country. The solution was to move the stash out to the United States. The problem was that the wealth consisted of shares of Seagram's, the liquor company (bootlegging is difficult without a source of booze). If the family were to sell the shares (and a moving of the shares out of Canada would be deemed a disposition), the tax bite would amount to about $700 million in capital gains. Their lawyers and accountants came up with a plan to use Canadian and U.S. trusts to move the shares out of Canada tax free. The financial wizards thought it prudent to get an advance tax ruling from Revcan, which saw through the scheme and refused to grant it tax-free status. The gurus massaged the scheme, resubmitted it, but there was no format that Revcan would accept. But then out of the blue a Canadian senator decides that a fireside chat with the upper bureaucrats at the Department of National Revenue would be instructive. This senator had the Bronfmans to thank for his appointment, and lo and behold Revcan re-examined the "two trust tango" and said it was kosher. A blow was struck for the financial freedom of Canada's long-suffering billionaires.

But then along came Harris. George Harris is a social activist in Winnipeg. He complained to the courts that his tax burden was being increased because the Bronfmans' had been reduced by $700 million. Revcan argued that Harris didn't have the right to drag the taxpayers' records into court because of — you guessed it — taxpayer confidentiality. Revcan's argument went along the lines of how can we expect brothel owners, drug dealers, and other low lifes to pay their taxes if the information they supplied went from the taxman to the crown attorney? For God's sake, they'd all be in jail. Then where would we be? Instead of their contributing to society, they'd be in jail, a drain on society. The argument does have some logic; however, as usual, the tax collectors weren't too concerned about the client — their fear was that an obvious odious scam had been allowed to be executed with their approval. The downside for CRA was enormous in that not only would its image be tarnished but also all the tax-challenged billionaires in Canada would be seeking the same exit.

Thankfully, the courts are still relatively independent in this country, and the judge wouldn't accept the confidentiality argument. You then had the tax collectors trying to justify why something that smells like ten-day-old fish can be presented by a senator and immediately be as odourless as a live lobster. The bizarre part of this sorry episode is that Revcan fought desperately to protect the identity of this group of plutocrats while being more than happy to drag Dion and Angelil through the mud. Maybe not so strange after all when you consider that in one case Revcan was going to be exposed of possible wrongdoing while in the other taxpayers could be encouraged to reach for their wallets. At last report, the matter was dragging on through the courts, but it is doubtful that the assets moved offshore to the United States will ever be redomiciled in Canada and the appropriate amounts of tax paid.

Regrettably, not many of us have access to a senator who'd be willing to chat up the folks at Revcan to see things our way. Your member of Parliament won't intercede on your behalf no matter how odious the behaviour of the tax authorities. He or she is just as terrified of them as you were before reading this book. As well, you have the situation where the taxing authority is an agent of the crown and hence believed to be above reproach.

But what about the other side of the coin? Suppose you have enemies in high places: will the Tax Act and the enforcers at CRA be used against you? You bet. Take the case of Stephen LeDrew. Oh, you may demur, not that Stephen LeDrew, head of the Liberal Party of Canada. Yep, one and the same.

LeDrew, while head of the Liberal Party, recommended to the Prime Minister of the time, Jean Chrétien, that he step down from that position at the next party convention. LeDrew felt that Chrétien's manner had become more imperial than democratic, as did many of the Liberal faithful. Their fear was that the scandals and imperial cover-ups might destroy the party and its chances of re-election. This even though the opposition parties had been successfully demonized by the Liberals to the extent that Ontario residents considered any party with western Canadian affiliations as an extension of al Qaeda. Therefore, the Liberals were the only electable party in the country's largest region.

The emperor, excuse me, Prime Minister, was not amused, entertained, or receptive to the idea of his abdication. I'm sure fitting punishments were considered, such as throwing LeDrew to the lions in Montreal's Olympic facilities, but then it was found that graft had led to their construction as substandard and probably unsafe for such spectacles. A much less public punishment was decided.

It was known that LeDrew had a tax debt outstanding and that Revcan had accepted a payment schedule that would retire the amount over time. All seemed to be well in the Kingdom of Canada until, without warning, Revcan demanded from LeDrew that he pay the amount owing immediately. Revcan knew of his financial circumstances since the payment program had been worked out on the basis of those circumstances. What were Revcan's concerns? Was Revcan worried that he would skip the country? He's a Canadian lawyer with a family and new wife and home. Hardly someone who would *Take His Money and Run.* No, it seems that turning against the Prime Minister is a major impairment of one's credit worthiness (take note all of you who may have considered voting other than Liberal in the next election and have money outstanding to CRA).

As the Prime Minister's Office and everyone else knew, demanding that the guy pay immediately from funds he didn't have would force him into bankruptcy. It did.

I know what you're thinking: there is a very tenuous link between the events of LeDrew abandoning the PM and the tax department forcing him into bankruptcy. Well, then, what about the fact that a reporter at the *Toronto Sun* was given all the facts by a mysterious source in the government? A reporter who, when approached by the Ottawa source, had dreams of another revelation of sleaze with regard to girlriends or expense accounts, revelations he'd received in the past. The details provided were explicit enough to have come only from within the government. However, put yourself in his position: is this a news story? Are you going to yell "Stop the presses!" Hardly — this is a dog bites man story. The problem facing the reporter was that, if he didn't publish all the stories provided by "deep nasal," he might not get any more.

What was the outcome? I for one would have been appalled had it been my information. If your most personal tax matters are going to be revealed by the government to the press, would you not expect it to be to a national paper such as the *Globe and Mail* or *National Post* rather than a tabloid? The only greater insult would have been to release the information through one of those free papers. I don't know how LeDrew felt, but I would have felt insulted.

More seriously, how did Revcan fare? Well, it had a deal where LeDrew would pay some $350,000 or so over time plus all that juicy interest Revcan charges. When it demanded immediate payment and the man had no assets with which to pay, he had to declare bankruptcy. At the bankruptcy hearing, Revcan was the only creditor (LeDrew owed nobody else anything of substance), and once in court what it wanted as well as money was information about a third party, LeDrew's wife. As you know from your reading so far, the Tax Act frowns on the gathering of third-party information. As well, there is the concept of taxpayer confidentiality. So there they are in court, and the government's lawyers are asking LeDrew to violate another taxpayer's confidentiality. The judge wasn't impressed. As for the payout, remember that LeDrew was unable to pay the lump sum, which was why Revcan had agreed to a payment schedule. Therefore, the tax collectors weren't about to get the total amount. So in the end, Revcan had to settle for an amount around three-quarters of the original debt. Ah, you say, we the people got screwed again since the amount not collected ended up on our tax bills.

It gets worse. Who paid the legal costs of this undertaking? In civil law, if you are offered a settlement of, let's say, $500,000 as a result of your claim against a defendant and you refuse it and proceed to court, then things get testy. If you win an amount greater than the amount offered, the court cost will be borne by the loser. If, however, the court awards you only $200,000 after you've turned down the original $500,000, then you'll end up paying court costs. That seems only logical since you've wasted the court's time. LeDrew had a settlement with Revcan, and as a result of the bankruptcy Revcan will receive less than the original amount. At the time of this writing, LeDrew was considering applying for costs, which of course you and I will have to pay if the judge awards them to him. If he is awarded costs, then the weapon of forced bankruptcies after payment has been agreed upon will no longer be used.

So what have you learned from all this? First, never admit that the emperor has no clothes. If you are going to make enemies in Ottawa, expect to have any of your secrets exposed. Now with csis having been given even greater powers of privacy invasion, you can imagine how dangerous the outcome could be. Second, taxpayer confidentiality applies only to the advantage of Revcan when dealing with low lifes or preventing you from questioning it. Therefore, don't depend on your information being kept confidential. At this point, you may believe that the Tax Act is used only to punish the wayward. Look at the following story, though, and determine who was punished and who was rewarded.

CHAPTER 14

Loopholes AHOY!

REVCAN'S CREATION OF SPECIAL CASES

Politics is a tough game. Horse trading is definitely out as most civilized countries frown on the trading of political favours. For example, I couldn't say, if I was your sitting MP, that if you deliver pizza for my campaign workers I will give you a Senate seat. But I can — nudge, nudge, wink, wink — say that if the pizza is forthcoming your future might hold some time spent in a red room in Ottawa. And so in Canada this is how political favours are meted out and tabs paid. Professional courtesy demands that, when the patronage is to be dispensed, you reward the opposition's bag men as well as your own. Similarly, if as the leader of the loyal opposition one of your MPs decides to audiotape the ruling party offering a political bribe to a member of the opposition, you would certainly put an end to that. We can't have MPs and party stalwarts heading for the slammer because of audio-recorded evidence. It's bad for business.

So what do you do when a potential suitor for the head of the opposition asks a favour? Well, of course, you oblige. He would do the same for you.

I don't know if a favour was asked for in this case, but let me tell you a story, and you be the judge. Once upon a time, there was a fairy kingdom where, although the people were poor, their kingdom was rich. For many years, the fairies living in the kingdom saw their income increase about 1.8% annually while the kingdom grew rich. This occurred because within the kingdom was a wealth-eating dragon called Taxman. It was very difficult for any of the fairies to get rich because the Taxman ate half their wealth and the excrement of this dragon was collected by the kingdom and kept as a pile called "surplus."

In the history of this strange place was the tale of a prince whose father almost became king. Alas, the father died without ever reaching the throne. Nothing too sinister here — just a problem with timing. At the time of the father's ascendancy to the throne, a new king was offered, and he caught the plebeians' eye, and this younger candidate was anointed king rather than the older gentleman. I am sure that the older prince's son was aghast that his father had been so disrespected after having served his time in the trenches. So I suspect that the son at some level wanted to right this perceived wrong. As you know in all fairy tales, at this point the aggrieved prince leaves the kingdom and goes far a field to amass a great fortune, which he intends to use to set right the perceived wrong. He had to go to distant lands where there was no dragon to eat wealth.

Now a problem arose. The prince's fortune was made and continues to be made in a tax haven by shipping with vessels that are not of the kingdom. If he were to repatriate the fortune, it would be sorely diminished by the great rapacious wealth-eating dragon, Taxman. If that were to happen, then the prince's ability to gain the throne stolen from his father might be jeopardized.

Now the prince was no dummy. He knew that his father's NGP (Natural Governing Party) was no longer ruling, so someone contacted the head of the currently ruling party, NNGP (Not the Natural Governing Party), and suggested that it would be a mark of courtesy to the opposition to provide a tax break to the prince so that he would be protected from the wealth-destroying dragon. In that way, the prince might be able to return to the kingdom and pursue the crown. The smarter elements of Not the Natural Governing Party realized that the prince could be the modern equivalent to the combative Mark Anthony to the current Octavius, who was lusting for power with the return of the Natural Governing Party. The current rulers recognized that any impediment to the seeker of the crown would be to their advantage, for they recognized their current opponent as a political killer. So, sure, let's put a muzzle on Taxman so that all the people who make their money from ships owned in offshore tax havens are not taxed in the kingdom. This is the only wealth Taxman cannot eat.

Note that the change was made only for people who make their money in shipping offshore. Not investments, eyeglass frame manufacture, or T-shirt monogramming offshore, just shipping. People who made money outside the country with vessels needn't have that income attributed to them in Canada. So if you were a Bermudian shipping

magnate and you decided to reside in Canada and snipe at
the sitting head of the opposition with the intent of pursuing his job, how convenient for everyone.

While Mulroney and the Conservatives were in power
in 1991, Section 250 of the Income Tax Act was changed so
that a foreign corporation controlled by a Canadian
wouldn't be deemed to have earned income in Canada and
hence be taxable in Canada if the source of the income was
international shipping. Just to be sure, Section 248 of the
act clarified that the St. Lawrence River and the Great
Lakes constituted part of the universe of international shipping. (This was for tax purposes only. Any foreign ships
entering those waters would be subject to Canadian law —
except tax law.) To ensure that shipping income would be
exempt under any circumstances, Section 81 of the act was
changed so that persons residing outside Canada wouldn't
be liable for tax on income earned in Canada from international shipping. The litmus test of Canadian taxation of
foreign companies has always been the "mind and management" test, which says that, if "mind and management"
rest in Canada, the corporation is Canadian and taxable in
Canada. That was thrown out for international shipping.

There must have been a near collision of ships with the
tax reef in 1994,[24] because in 1995 the act had to be changed
again (enacted in 1998 but made retroactive to 1995, probably to protect some income) so that capital gains made by
those foreign international shipping corporations controlled
by Canadians wouldn't be subject to capital gains taxation
should they sell a ship for a tax-free profit. Whew, a close call.

---

[24] A deemed disposition subject to capital gains tax occurred when the ships
were redomiciled from Bermuda to the Barbados.

These changes allowed Paul Martin Jr. to manage his shipping empire from Canada without being taxed on its offshore profits. He could thus return to Canada and be an ongoing source of annoyance to then head of the Liberal Party, Jean Chrétien, the Genghis Khan of Canadian politicians. When you think about it, this was a brilliant piece of political seamanship. The Conservatives had provided a political favour to the upcoming star in the Liberal ranks while at the same time providing an inconvenience to the leader of their competitors.

In justifying these changes, the Department of Finance claimed that it would increase Canada's position and status in international shipping. Note that the ships do not have to be built or registered in Canada, nor do they have to crewed by Canadians. I am still puzzled how this is going to change Canada's presence, because all these boats are foreign owned (they have to be to remain free of tax). But then again why would anyone want Canada to have a presence in international shipping if the boats weren't built here or don't provide employment for Canadian seamen?

Those of you with a financial bent are likely asking what good did all this do for the prince since his fortune was offshore and not available to provide ladders for ascendancy to the crown. Thankfully, a little tinkering allowed the use of exempt surplus rules to have the funds arrive in Canada without having been gnawed by the tax dragon. And that, readers, is how the faithful prince managed to defeat the wealth-destroying dragon and regain the kingdom denied his father.

This must be a fairy tale, since how else could there be changes in the Income Tax Act that would benefit so few people? An equivalent piece of legislation might be along the lines of all Canadians who write books critical of the tax system will be taxed only on their income from the practice of neural surgery. But then we do have legislation that allows the head of the government and the opposition to have free housing in Ottawa without being deemed to have a taxable benefit derived from their employment, benefits that accrue to only two people.

One result of these changes is that people who were not in the international shipping business but were wealthy started speaking in nautical terms, such as "It looks like the Liberals have taken a list to port. They should belay any thoughts of more health care for the swabs." At the same time, they became active in international shipping, so that many of the best clubs now sound like a Halifax dock.

I have always wondered how the changes to the Tax Act regarding shipping arose. Did someone ask for them? Was it some sort of mistake? I think the next change should be for the benefit of tax book authors.

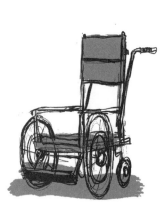

CHAPTER 15

Are You NUTS?

THE SHAMEFUL PERSECUTION OF THE DISABLED

As Samuel Goldwyn said when told that one of his stars couldn't be on the lot because she was seeing her psychiatrist, "Anyone who sees a psychiatrist should have his head examined." But what if you really are permanently disabled, is there not some relief in the Tax Act? Yes, there is, but like Oliver Twist's jam it is available yesterday and tomorrow but seldom today. The problem lies particularly with the mentally impaired.

If you are disabled, you can use form T2201 for an application for a Disabled Tax Credit. It doesn't amount to a lot of money, but for someone who has lost his or her earning capacity it can help by relieving some of the tax burden on the reduced income the unfortunate person is receiving. The form is easy enough when you are dealing with physical disabilities, but it becomes a nightmare for the person who wants to make an application as a result of mental disability.

I often listen to sad tales of patients who have had their lives derailed by some form of mental illness or other. It isn't difficult for me to envision that people who have developed a fear of crowds or confined spaces would have trouble in the modern work world. And what about us paranoids?

Form T2201, page 7, deals with the question of mental impairment with a number of generalized questions, which the practitioner must answer in one set of boxes "yes" or "no." The whole field of psychoanalysis is reduced to one question. To make things worse, CRA has taken a very adversarial stance with respect to the medical profession with regard to people who make this application citing a mental disability, to the extent that some medical practitioners are reluctant to fill in the form, fearing harassment from Revcan.

For example, one of the questions is "Does the individual have the ability to think, perceive and remember?" This question has no medical basis. If you are a medical person, you are going to think carefully about including that question as part of your "yes" response because it is meaningless, and you could therefore be challenged. Physicians have been advised by Revcan to "answer no only if and when their patient cannot manage or initiate their own personal care without constant supervision." That to me seems like a very restrictive definition of mental impairment.

As you can well imagine, the judges hearing these cases, when confronted by someone in the agony of a mental illness, are not likely to stretch to reach a decision in favour of the tax collectors. One of the most famous cases involves

Dennis Radage, who appeared before Judge Bowman in 1996. The judge diligently considered that the meaning of the abilities to *think, perceive,* and *remember,* while not nonexistent in the patient, were sufficiently limited to bring him within the guidelines. I personally don't like the judgment because it places the onus on the judge to determine a medical condition.

The *Buchanan* case offered more complexities in that the patient was diagnosed as having affective bipolar disorder. This insidious condition allows the patient to function quite well at some level, but with remaining thought processes that are impaired. The doctor who diagnosed the patient chose to interpret that the six items used by CRA[25] were all-inclusive. In that way, there is a high threshold placed before the patient. Judge Campbell, hearing the case, said that they are not to be read together but that each action is considered separately. Revcan wouldn't accept that interpretation and asked the Attorney General of Canada to appeal the decision to the Federal Court of Appeal. At the time of this writing, I hadn't heard the outcome of that appeal.

Those of you who remember your logic courses will recall the test that, for the proposition to be true, "a and b and c and d . . ." have to be true. This places a high threshold on the proposition. As a result, if you read the form T2201,[26] logic would dictate that, unless you want the benefit to be impossible to obtain, you wouldn't require the criteria to be all-inclusive.

My conclusion is that once again the intent of Parliament with respect to providing some relief to the

[25] See the Tax Act, Section 118.4(1)(c)
[26] http://www.cra-arc.gc.ca/E/pbg/tf/t2201/README.html

unfortunates of this country has been overridden by the rapaciousness of the tax-collecting bureaucrats. The subtleties of what constitutes mental impairment cannot be reduced to a one-answer question. The state has admitted this in the efforts it expends on the question of the state of mind of a criminal at the time of the commission of a crime.

I was once the patient of a doctor who got harassed out of his profession because there were those who felt that he placed too many patients on the disability lists. Any doctor looking at form T2201 would quickly conclude that his judgment of a person's disabilities could easily be disputed. Hence, there is a reluctance to supply patients with a completed form. The mental health professionals have, for the past four years, lobbied to get the form changed, and it remains in its past format. Sadly, the Disability Tax Credit is probably unavailable to the mentally impaired.

If you are considering applying for the Disability Tax Credit for a person who is mentally disabled, then you are facing an uphill battle as even the medical practitioners are reluctant to use the form T2201 for anything but physical disabilities.

CHAPTER 16

Time's UP!

....

REVCAN'S ATTEMPT TO UNLIMIT LIMITATIONS

Who is Joe Markevich? You may think that Joe is some sort of Cold War warrior; Joe is indeed a warrior, but of a later genre, and he is a victor.

Joe Markevich was, in the 1980s, a successful mining promoter in British Columbia. He filed his taxes but began to fall behind in his payments. As you can imagine, there is no source deduction for income tax at the stock exchange floor. In 1986, he was assessed as owing back taxes to Revcan. Markevich's house was sold, and the proceeds were used to cover a portion of the debt, leaving $267,437.61 outstanding. In 1987, the boys and girls in collections concluded that they had tapped out poor old Joe and that there was little chance of collecting the balance due, so they wrote off the debt.

From 1992 on, Joe paid his income taxes as they accrued and was shown at times to have a zero balance owing. In 1995, he started to fall behind again in his tax payments, and Revcan went on to issue orders to people doing business with Joe to pay it any funds that might otherwise go to him. Noting that Joe had an income again, Revcan sent him a bill for $770,583.42, consisting of the original amount owing from 1987 and $503,145.81 in interest.

Now remember that Revcan had over the years since 1987 told Joe he had no taxes owing. It had written off the debt. Now, eight years later, it had decided to "unwrite it off."

Joe went to court with his lawyers, arguing that there was a statute of limitations issue regarding Revcan's demand. His lawyers said that after six years the Revcan claim was extinguished because it had passed beyond the statute of limitations. These rules are in place to force people with criminal or civil issues to pursue redress in a reasonable period or move on.

Revcan argued that there was no statute of limitations mentioned in the Income Tax Act and thus one could not be applied. Joe's lawyers said that, because the feds were doing business in the provinces, the provincial statutes would apply.[27] When the smoke cleared, $1.26 billion (yes, that is billion) of debts due to the crown from GST, royalties, income tax, et cetera, which have not been pursued

---

[27] I have read the court file and noted that the Revcan lawyers side-stepped the issue of the legitimacy of the Tax Act and the province's sole right to direct taxation.

for a period beyond your provincial statute of limitations, is now extinguished.

What did it mean for you? If you had an old debt to Revcan that wasn't in collection for a period of more than six years, it was likely uncollectible. Not to be denied the ability to collect because of its sloppiness, and to put Revcan in a position to regain what it had lost, the Minister of National Revenue had new legislation passed in 2003. Under the new rules, Revcan gave itself ten years in which it had to step up to the plate, and it made the legislation retroactive. I could tell from their bluish tinge that some civil liberties lawyers I spoke to were upset by the retroactive aspect of the new legislation. Can you imagine your local municipality coming up to you and saying "We have just passed a no-parking rule on the street in front of your house, and by the way you are guilty of violating it because we put it into effect as of 1945."

The other change that Revcan made was to have any efforts, such as writing to the potential tax debtor, stand as justification for maintaining the debt even if formal collection hadn't been instituted. This new legislation, with its retroactive application and odious differences from other civil legislation regarding statutes of limitations, is bound to be challenged in the future. As well, don't be surprised if everybody in Canada starts getting Christmas cards from Revcan. That way it can claim that its contact with the taxpayer was constant.

However, for the taxpayer, it means that, if Revcan hasn't undertaken collection for a period of ten years from the origin of the debt, it may still be able to pursue you. At least you'll have ten years to get your assets out of the country!

CHAPTER 17

Grrr to GAAR

·······························

REMINDING REVCAN THAT AVOIDANCE IS NOT EVASION

No, I am not talking about some *Star Wars* characters here. These are beasts that roam unfettered in our Tax Act.

GAAR, or the "general anti-avoidance rules" (Section 245 of the ITA), says that, if a taxpayer undertakes a commercial action the sole purpose of which is to reduce his tax payable, then CRA has the option of reversing the transaction. I'll bet you are wondering why Revcan hasn't come after you about those flow through shares[28] shares you bought or that contribution you made to your RRSP. If you think back to some early discourse on the subject of tax

[28] Flow through shares allow the company issuing them to assign the write-offs for exploration work to be claimed by the shareholders against their personal income.

avoidance, you'll remember the House of Lords ruling that said a man has the right to arrange his financial affairs in such a manner as to attract the least amount of tax (*Inland Revenue v. Westminster,* 1938). Many of the Commonwealth countries were dominions or attached to the United Kingdom in such a way that what became British law applied in the colony, dominion, or whatever. In 1938, Canada was a dominion, so that little piece of jurisprudence applied here. It has always caused much consternation among our tax collectors. As I mentioned in previous discourse on that ruling, the important utterance from the law lords was that a "man" had the right. Revcan has taken that literally and used its anti-avoidance rule with gusto against corporations and other legal entities but has shied away from the "man."

The reason is the very same one that has caused all that hand-wringing and garment-rending in the United Kingdom. Had the UK tax authorities not taken it upon themselves to tackle the Lord of Westminster on some of his tax-avoiding ways with his real estate empire in London, a nasty precedent might not have been set. Once enshrined as the law of the land, it is impossible to get around.

Try this on for GAAR size. A lawyer named Singleton went to his law partners and said, "Hey, guys, I want to sell my share of the partnership. What's it worth?" His partners priced it at $300,000. Mr. Singleton took his $300,000 and went to his local bank and said he wanted to pay off the mortgage on his house. The bank said fine.

Now bear in mind that the interest of about $15,000 per year on Mr. Singleton's mortgage was not tax deductible, being a personal expense. So he had eliminated $15,000 of personal expenses. But he no longer owned a piece of a law partnership. Mr. Singleton decided he liked being a partner rather than a wage slave, so he asked his previous partners if they had a partnership available and what the cost would be. They replied that he could buy a partnership in his old firm for $300,000.

Mr. Singleton's personal balance sheet looked pretty good to his bank since he now owned a house without a mortgage, so when he asked the bank for a loan of $300,000 to buy into a law partnership the bank said fine. He walked over to his previous partners and handed them a cheque for $300,000 and sat down at his old desk. All in the course of a day.

Mind you the interest on the $300,000 that he had borrowed to buy the partnership was a tax deductible expense because Singleton was deriving revenue as a result of having invested the money in a business asset. Mr. Singleton was richer by $15,000 per year.

The boys and girls at Revcan weren't amused. They'd seen this sort of hanky panky before. Merchants would reduce their inventory and apply the proceeds to their personal loans, that sort of thing, and Revcan would grumble GAAR. The merchant would tuck his tail between his legs and plead for mercy, and life would go on as before, with all of the merchant's personal capital tied up in his business, keeping his tax deductible expenses low and his personal nondeductible financial expenses high.

When Revcan went after Singleton, he scoffed. The arrogance of our tax collectors who have all the rules tilted in their favour knows no bounds. They didn't take well to that sort of behaviour and decided to pursue Singleton. It also seems that their common sense was a little in short supply. Had it been me, and knowing that this guy was a lawyer and probably hadn't undertaken this sleight of hand without some research, I would have just backed off and prayed that taxpayer confidentiality would keep it all under wraps. Nobody but Singleton and the tax collectors would know. Instead, they thought they could bludgeon the guy into submission with legal costs. What does a lawyer like? Legal bills. He lives off them. So off they went to the Supreme Court, and the justices ruled in Singleton's favour, and now everybody is doing it.

Revcan pleaded that the whole thing took place in the course of a day and was obviously a pure tax avoidance scheme. Well, so are RRSPs a tax avoidance scheme. The logic that prevailed on the bench was that, if it wasn't illegal, it wasn't a problem. But what about GAAR? Saner heads at Revcan prevailed. Proceeding down a track that had chopped the legs out from under one of its best weapon bearers wasn't a good idea. If Revcan tried anything further, it might lose even more ground. I'll bet that on the day of the Singleton judgment a flat tax even started to look good to Revcan.

What does it mean for you? If you are in a business, you can sell off your inventory and apply the proceeds to your personal finances and then refinance your business with debt that has tax deductible interest. If you are in a profession, you can refinance your part of the profession and apply the funds to your home and watch it grow tax free as a principal residence while your indebted business assets, which are subject to capital gains tax, are weighted with debt.

CHAPTER 18

REOP, SHBOOM, SHBOOM

REVCAN'S GREED FOR YOUR "PROFITS"

Those of you old enough to remember Ella Fitzgerald and her jazz singing will recall "beop, doodlyday, sheban," but probably can't recall any of her songs using the word REOP. However, when you listen to the wailing of the dudes down at the tax office, the music sounds like country and western bemoaning the loss of REOP. Who, you might ask, was the lovely REOP that her loss was so soul searing for the lads at Revcan? REOP was one of the many rules that had to exist to avoid the use of corporate rules for the benefit of the individual. REOP stands for "reasonable expectation of profit." To the best of my recollection, it all started on the farm.

In the early 1950s, the horsey set of Canada would buy little farms where they would retire for the summer away from the heat of the city and enjoy their equestrian pursuits. The ever-vigilant eyes of Revcan noticed that none of these farms ever made any money for tax purposes but had huge write-offs. After a number of years, the tax guys concluded that there was never a reasonable expectation of profit and attributed the write-offs back to the owners as personal expenses and hence un-deductible. So far so good, but what about real estate?

If an investor buys a property and rents it out and charges the depreciation and all the expenses associated with the property, he is likely to run at a loss. At the end of his investment over, say, fifteen years, he will probably sell the property with a huge gain and pay an immense tax. But in the intervening years, he has managed to report a loss every year. The reason for the loss was the noncash charge for depreciation of the building. Although the amount charged in the statements isn't paid out, it's a legitimate expense for tax purposes. This noncash charge has been the basis for many a real estate empire. However, some people went too far, and Revcan went for the jugular.

This opened up the whole concept of REOP to scrutiny. Arguments were raised such as what about J.K. Rowling and the years she worked on the first Harry Potter book? Should she have been allowed to deduct her expenses? In Canada, probably not. This has always been a bone of contention for Canadian authors. Apparently, there are literary critics in the tax department who can judge whether a book will be a success or a failure even before the manuscript hits the publisher's desk. Take this book, for example. Upon review, the folks at Revcan would give it the green light for tax write-offs since they would be big buyers.

What happened to REOP? In the end, it looked like Saint

Sebastian with all the arrows sticking out of him. The Supreme Court of Canada just kept on shooting; Revcan kept trying to revive it, but the beast was mortally wounded. The old REOP was dead — long live the new REOP!

The death started with the first wound inflicted by the *Ludco* case in 2001. The taxpayer held shares on margin with the interest costs of $6 million and earned dividend income of $600,000. Revcan wanted to disallow the interest expense as a deduction, but the taxpayer went to the Supreme Court of Canada (SCC), which then had the audacity to review the Income Tax Act. The act says that interest is deductible where the borrowing was made "for the purpose of earning income." The SCC concluded that income didn't mean a profit — you just had to make money. Thinking about it, that is a reasonable conclusion. Who is to say what amount of income is appropriate? The taxpayers had their interest expense retained as a deduction against income.

While REOP was lying in the gutter licking its wounds after the beating it had received at the hands of the Ludcos and their lawyers, along came Brian Stewart to put the boots to it in 2002. Stewart bought condominiums that he would lever with borrowed money with the anticipation of selling them at some point in the future with a capital gain. With the combination of depreciation and interest expense, the enterprise generated $58,000 in losses. CRA disallowed the loss on the basis that there was no reasonable expectation of profit. This issue went to the SCC, and the justices decided that "the REOP test should not be accepted as the test to determine whether a taxpayer's activities constitute a source of income" — in other words, a business. According to the SCC, "the motivation of capital gains accords with the ordinary business person's understanding of 'pursuit of profit' and may be taken into account to determine whether the taxpayer's activity is commercial in nature." Stewart got his deductions. REOP was taken from where it lay and put on life-support systems. Revcan was determined not to have it die no matter how badly it had been abused by a bunch of lawyers and Supreme Court justices.

As with a human life-support system, the picture is not pretty. There have to be tubes and monitors and special equipment. The same applies to a simple tax rule such as REOP that is near death. The body lying there is much more complicated than before it was wounded. Revcan adopted new rules. They state that a taxpayer will only be allowed to deduct losses for a given year if, in that year, it is reasonable to assume that the taxpayer will realize a cumulative profit from the investment during the time it is held. I'll bet when the tax lawyers saw that bit of legislation their hearts skipped a beat. As well as the extension to the summer cottage and a new Porsche, their thoughts would have been along the line of what is a "reasonable" assumption that the taxpayer will realize a profit? Or how about the time that a taxpayer holds the investment? Does infinity count? Even more interesting is that the new rules specifically exclude capital gains as an expected profit. Wow! Capital gains are no longer profits (except for taxation purposes).[29] Wait till the lawyers get to work on that one.

---

[29] This reminds me of the personal property rules. If you own a Ferrari, and sell it for a profit, the amount is taxable. If you sell it at a loss, the amount is not deductible. Huh?

CHAPTER 19

Home, Bitter HOME

HOW NOT TO BE A CANADIAN RESIDENT

One of the most effective tax avoidance systems involves changing your residency. Canada, like most countries, but unlike the United States, bases tax liability on residency. If you are resident in a country, then you are liable for taxation because you consume services in that country, according to the Canadian model. The United States, on the other hand, bases taxation on citizenship. If you are a citizen of the United States, then you are liable for income tax in that country irrespective of where you live.[30] This causes headaches not only for the individuals but also for

[30] In the United States, if you give up your residency for tax purposes, the IRS can extend your citizenship for another ten years even if you have joined al Qaeda.

foreign governments, which have to extract tax from American citizens living in their countries while the taxpayers are forking money over to the U.S. Internal Revenue Service. For the Canadian citizen, life is much simpler.

If a Canadian severs his ties with Canada and moves abroad, then he is no longer liable for income tax in Canada. Now you understand why the Irvings, deGroots, and Stronachs all live somewhere else — not to mention lesser financial gods. To sever his ties, a Canadian cannot have a residence, spouse, car, driver's licence, bank account, club membership, et cetera in Canada. He has to give up his provincial health care and rely on private foreign hospital insurance. None of these things is onerous, and in some cases, such as hospital insurance, the former taxpayer finds himself in a beneficial position compared with his Canadian resident counterpart.[31] Many Canadians established residency in places such as Holland and Ireland where they took their pensions without tax and enjoyed a beneficial tax regime. Others took jobs in the oil-rich countries and received spectacular tax-free salaries. So far, so good. What happens if, for some unforeseen reason, the Canadian or one of his immediate family members returns to the old sod? The first instance of this that I can find occurred in the 1950s.

There was a case where a Newfoundland merchant mariner had been at sea for more than five years, never setting foot in Canada. Obviously, he had severed all ties as he consumed none of what the Canadian government had on

---

[31] When I lived offshore, I had hospital insurance for about $3,000 a year, which covered me for U.S. $1.5 million in hospitalization as soon as I needed it. No waiting for me, even for elective surgery.

offer. When he returned, Revcan went after him for back taxes. His defence was that he hadn't resided in Canada for the five years in question. Revcan's argument was that he hadn't established a new residence and therefore was *resident in the last place of permanent residency.* His last permanent residence was Canada. Revcan prevailed. Well, that was a good rule for Revcan until in recent years people have left Canada for a multitude of reasons. Some of these individuals established a residency in another country, worked there, and then went on extended holidays, giving up their most recent residency. Some who returned were then told by Revcan that, seeing as for a period they had no permanent residency, they were by default residents of Canada.

What happened to that ruling about people with no current residency being resident in their last country of residence? Without a lawyer to find that and plead it in court for $50,000, it becomes of little help to the man on the street.

Revcan has tried in many cases to dispute the period of nonresidency. Its best outcome would be to say that the ten years you were living and working in Saudi Arabia, not using the free health care or education available in Canada (the major reason given by the majority of immigrants for choosing Canada as a destination), you were actually resident in Canada. If Revcan prevails, you can't bill Ontario for the kidney transplant you may have got from Saudi Arabia, nor can you get the cost of schooling your children in England. You would, however, be liable for income tax.

These challenges are often based on the answers the Canadian gave on the departure form, NR 73. If the Canadian wants an immediate resolution of his residency status, he must file the NR 73 form and receive an adjudication of his residency status. Interestingly, according to Revcan, its opinion isn't binding. Nevertheless, if one wants an immediate, even if temporary, status opinion, the NR 73[32] has to be provided. Among the questions is one asking if you will be liable for income tax in your new country of residency. What arrogance! I can imagine the answer given by new residents of, say, Saudi Arabia or the Turks and Caicos Islands. "Yes, sir. I tried desperately to pay income tax to the government, but they adamantly refused to accept it. They state it would start an ugly precedent." So does this negate your nonresidency in Canada because you can't pay income tax in your new residence?

Not necessarily, because Revcan informs me that it uses a "mosaic" approach. If the parts of your life fitted together imply foreign residence, then you are accepted as being nonresident. Obviously, some parts of the mosaic are bigger than others and thus more significant as part of the entire picture. A spouse left behind is one of the biggies. In recent years, however, the courts have taken a much more enlightened attitude about why and when a spouse can be in Canada and the wage earner can claim to be nonresident.

The most interesting case involved a man named Emain Kadrie. Revcan claimed that, as a result of Kadrie having

(a) Canadian citizenship,

(b) a Canadian passport,

(c) a Canadian driver's licence,

(d) an address in Canada,

(e) maintained a rented apartment in Canada,

---

[32] http://www.cra-arc.gc.ca/E/pbg/tf/nr73/README.html

(f) sent his children to school in Canada, and

(g) a wife in Canada,

he was therefore a resident of Canada.

At first glance, I, like you, would think that these pieces of the mosaic pretty well defined Mr. Kadrie as a resident of Canada. His lawyer argued the issue in Tax Court using the *Thomson v. Minister of National Revenue* case heard in the Supreme Court of Canada. In that landmark case, the courts ruled that a man was resident "in the place where in the settled routine of his life he regularly, normally or customarily lives." What the court said was that you are resident where you live and your life unfolds. Mosaics are nice, but they should be kept to floors and walls and out of people's lives.

I wonder how this case ever got this far, because when you hear the details common sense would tell you that Kadrie didn't live in Canada. More importantly, when he left Canada, he had severed all ties. What happened after his departure muddied his residency picture.

Kadrie left Canada in 1977 to work for an employer in Kuwait. He continued to work for that employer until returning to Canada in 1994. In September of 1990, he sent his family to Canada as a result of the impending invasion of Kuwait by Iraq. He continued to work for his Kuwaiti employer, but from offices in New York and Dubai, and then returned to his company-provided apartment in Kuwait after hostilities had ended. His wife was fearful of returning to Kuwait, and there were impediments to her returning. Therefore, the apartment, schooling, and wife in Canada were out of necessity rather than choice. Importantly, Kadrie hadn't left a spouse behind; she had returned from Kuwait after an extended period there. The address he maintained in Canada was his parents' home and allowed for a permanent address for mail purposes during the turmoil of the conflict and its aftermath.

I mentioned that the facts when viewed in hindsight certainly give the impression of a nonresident. I wonder if the Revcan employees looked at the other "mosaic," which gave a very clear indication of a man living and working in Kuwait while his family out of necessity sought refuge in Canada. I suspect they were overawed by the presence of Mrs. Kadrie in Canada. Again, it was a situation that shouldn't have been allowed to go to court because Revcan should have realized that if the taxpayer was going to fight there was a chance of his winning, and that would diminish the tax collector's power. What was lost in this case was the ability to use the spouse's presence in Canada as a pre-eminent defining factor of residency for the taxpayer. As well, this and the *Thomson* case rulings in favour of the defendants have negated the mosaic approach and placed the emphasis on the facts of the individual's residency, not on the ancillary matters such as his having a driver's licence in Canada. As well, it is excessive to imply that a Canadian citizen should give up his passport and citizenship to be able to work or live abroad.

In Kadrie's case, the emphasis from Revcan's view was the attachments to Canada, issues that weren't everyday parts of his life. A similar case involved Mr. Min Shan Shih, where the everyday aspects of his life were ignored by the tax collectors, and in this instance tangential issues were used to define his Canadian residency.

Again the biggie for Revcan was the spouse. Min Shan Shih was a dentist employed in Taiwan, a member of a church congregation and tennis club there. He had a Taiwan driver's licence and was a member of the Taiwan Pharmaceutical Society. He filed a tax return in Canada on minor amounts of investment income in 1991 through 1994. The confusing part for Revcan was that he used an address in Regina, Saskatchewan, where his wife and three sons were staying. Their presence was a result of the boys attending a private school in the area. Note that Mr. Min wasn't using the public school system. The Tax Court ruled against Revcan, noting that the *Thomson* case precedent certainly indicated that the substance of Mr. Min's life was in Taiwan. The court also ruled that the use of an address in mailings shouldn't be used to bias the residency question.

There are two important issues in these cases. First, from the Kadrie case, if you resume your residency after a period of working abroad, be aware that the tax collector is going to look for a weakness in your nonresidency claim. The first and most obvious shield is to be prepared for scrutiny and be able to protect the weakest links in the chain. Second, if you bear in mind that tax collection is a business, and if you can make the case that there is little to be gained from you, then Revcan may pass on pursuing you. If you bank abroad, lease rather than own, and have little in the way of domestic income, then the judicious action by Revcan is to look for other geese to pluck. Remember what triggered its interest — the return to Canada.

In prehistoric times, a mailing address was very important to most everybody, including Revcan. If, as in my case, you were sailing around in a yacht, the use of a multitude of addresses was only natural. This gave the tax collectors a variety of addresses from which to choose, and doubtless they choose the address most beneficial to them.

Today, address is very different. With call display on your phone, you can't be sure if the number you are seeing shows the area code of the place where the call actually originated. As well, the address most people will ask you for today is your e-mail address. If you are moving off-shore, just as a precaution, I'd give up an e-mail server or provider that had the suffix .ca. While living outside Canada, never send mail with a return address in Canada — and definitely not to the tax collectors. As you have seen, the courts have come into modern times and regard mailing addresses with less of an impact than Revcan attached to them in the past. But why take chances by using a Canadian address?

You may be asked by Revcan if your departure from Canada is tax driven. Should that question arise, I would, as Claude Rains said in the movie *Casablanca* upon hearing that there was clandestine gambling in Humphrey Bogart's establishment, respond that you are "shocked, shocked, shocked" to hear that you are no longer eligible to pay into Canada's coffers.

Residency is going to become an important issue for many Canadians because we have skills that are highly sought after abroad. As well, the greying of Canada will mean that there will be an increasing number of us who will want to retire to warm climes or undertake a more peripatetic lifestyle. This offers a superb opportunity for tax planning.[33] As a result, Revcan doesn't know whether you are tax avoiding or just travelling. Therefore, if you step out of Canada, know your tax consequences, and don't expect to return without some scrutiny.

[33] See my book *Take Your Money and Run.*

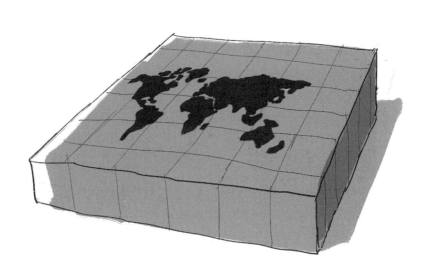

CHAPTER 20

God Save the TAX SYSTEM

RECREATING THE FLAT WORLD

After reading the previous chapters, you will have concluded, as I have, that the structure and administration of our tax system is a sorry mess. The least appealing course would be to try to save the existing system by repairing it. Some of you may have tried to restore an old house. The renovation consists of tearing out a lot of old plumbing and wiring. Also, there is the heating system to replace. In the end, you have a house with special boxes along walls to hide plumbing and ducts. You have sump pumps and special drainage, and the house is still expensive to operate and in continual need of upkeep. Why not just build a new house to look like the old one? Usually because of zoning laws and other community needs that disallow you to do so. I remember a man in Toronto who was denied a demolition permit for a house. He built a new house around the old one and then removed the old house from within. There are two routes for the Tax Act. Renovate it, or tear it down.

Renovation is the least acceptable route. If we were to undertake it, the first step would be a mechanism to stop the commingling of audits and investigations. The mechanism would be along the lines of requiring Revcan to decide at the outset if it is going to investigate or audit a taxpayer. Having made that choice, it would be unable to change tack. There would be howls and screams from Revcan. "What can we do having found flagrant violations of the Tax Act during an audit? Just ignore them?" Of course. Remember that discoveries made during an audit are by law precluded from use in an investigation. The taxman would say, of course, that he wouldn't use that exact information in the investigation — he'd find some other tangential evidence to hang the guy with. Right. He got his lead from an audit from which the taxpayer has no protection, and now that he has the scent obtained by the audit he wants to pursue an investigation. Not kosher.

The solution is simple. If Revcan starts an audit, then all information up to the date of the audit is privileged and cannot be used for any purpose but an audit. The tax collectors would then be barred from any investigation of and use of any information from before the date of the audit. Just think of what would have happened in the Cowell/ Dial Drugs case. The investigators wouldn't have been brought in, and Revcan would have collected back taxes on $260,000 of undeclared income and penalties. Instead, the investigators had a tainted case, and in the end the judge stayed the charges, and Revcan ended up with nothing, zilch. Of course, the same applies to Donovan and his four wrongs, not to mention Saplys and his $250,000 judgment against Revcan.

Revcan would fight such a change. The major objective of the investigation is to get that conviction that it can blab to the papers. From this, you are supposed to be frightened enough to comply with its every demand. Without the leads provided by audits, there would be fewer investigations and hence fewer convictions to announce to Canadian Press, Reuters, and the Christian Science Monitor. But then leads are not supposed to be provided by audits and investigations not inspired by taxpayer prominence — nudge, nudge, wink, wink.

Bearing in mind that tax collection is a business, let's run it like a business. If the tax company screws up, it should have to pay. If the bank pursues you for an erroneous amount, you have the option of suing it. Why not Revcan? In the short term, there would be a reduction in Revcan's total operating budget if tenuous cases when lost saw Revcan paying costs. It just wouldn't pursue anything but a rock-solid undertaking. As well, forget about pursuing people for political reasons, because, if one of those pursuits backfires and there is a judgment, it could be horrendous.

And what about money laundering? Let's say I've got this cat house, crack joint, bookie operation, or whatever. After I pay my taxes, I am free to spend my money on whatever I choose. Remember, the taxman is your silent partner. If your business is pimping and you give money to your partner, what is his business? Pimping. Are you really saying that kiddies' schooling should be paid for off the backs of enslaved women or addicted youths?

As a result of taxpayer confidentiality, you can pursue any manner of criminal activity and not be exposed to the authorities. Try it. Just answer the question on your tax form about "occupation" with "assassin." No questions except how much did you earn? Remember Mrs. MacDonald and her cute little Vancouver whorehouse? Occupation? Madam.

If Revcan exposed the criminals who file tax forms to the police, the incidence of crime in this country would go down. Crime would become a lot more expensive and therefore less desirable as an occupation. Let's follow my drug-delivering lad through his rounds. He arrives at the dealer's door and says, "Listen, I've had to raise my rates by fifty percent because I can no longer pass my earnings through the tax system."

The dealer says, "Hey, I should get a discount because you no longer have a partner to support."

"Sorry, not so. My money laundering charges are higher because I have to use a guy at a bakery uptown. He takes fifty percent, whereas Revcan took only thirty-five percent. As well, my security costs have gone up because I end up with too much cash hanging around."

"My customers can't afford to pay a hike like this. You are going to cost me sales."

The courier replies, "Sorry, I don't make the rules. Maybe you should write your MP."

The end result is that there would be fewer drugs consumed in the downtown core. If cracking down on money laundering will protect the state from terrorists, why won't penalizing the criminals with the same sort of financial rigour not diminish street crime?

The money-laundering rules were set up among other things to make crime more costly and hence less economically inviting. Crime has not stopped in Canada because of these rules. More likely the growth rate slowed. It has just become more expensive as more elegant ways have to be found to recycle the profits. The bizarre part is that government suppresses crime with these rules on the one hand and facilitates it through taxpayer confidentiality on the other.

If we are going to have taxpayer confidentiality, then let's get serious. Situations such as the Gernhart case, where her most private information was blabbed into the court records available at forty cents a copy, have got to end. If I give Revcan my records, then they should be barred from going anywhere but its offices. As well, it's time we got the politicians out of the tax business.

I don't know and probably never will know for sure if the tax investigators were spurred on by our political masters to see Tim Issac "punished" for helping Pat Landers lose the St. John's riding seat. Even the party faithful appear to be subject to the wrath of the Liberal leader. Stephen LeDrew, a long-time high-profile Liberal, advocated too early that Prime Minister Jean Chrétien retire and found himself being hounded by the taxman. As well, who knows which Canadian senator, if any, blew in the ear of the Minister of National Revenue with regard to whether or not the Bronfmans would be allowed to move their billions out of Canada tax free. I'll never know how the Tax Act was changed to allow Bermudian shipping magnates to avoid tax on their offshore earnings. But all these things came to pass. We need more rules at Revcan. The one I advocate is that the Minister of Revenue be forbidden to hear any reference or be involved in any discussion that involves a specific taxpayer. Also, the minister should be disallowed from mentioning a taxpayer's name to any deputy minister or employee of the department. The minister is there to count the revenue, not administer the Tax Act or discuss the tax matters of individual taxpayers.

The income tax system allows the government to use fiscal policy as a social engineering tool. Tax breaks are allocated on the basis of driving people into some sort of socially beneficial pursuit. Remember how we were going to preserve Canadian culture with the tax-driven movie production? Many of those films are resting where they should, on some producer's shelf. However, the shelf is located in very fancy accommodations as a result of being able to sell overblown tax credits to doctors and dentists.

Now, without government social engineering, Canada is growing a domestic cadre of experienced, competent people capable of making world-class movies right on your main street (there is a lot of government engineering, especially tax credits in Ontario and British Columbia). If you live in one of the larger cities of Canada, you will see movies being made on your streets daily. Admittedly, these are foreign companies, but they are developing a local expertise. Could a different tax system spur on that process? No, but neither did the graduated income tax.

CHAPTER 21

The Seventeen
PERCENT SOLUTION

···

CLEANING UP THE MESS AT REVCAN

At a recent lunch as the guest of a well-known Canadian tax lawyer who consults to the Department of Finance and who had given me and many more Canadians some sage advice on tax avoidance, he said that he was beginning to feel sorry for the folks at the tax department. He pointed out that the courts were more frequently ruling against Revcan. As well, decisions at the Supreme Court level effectively tied the hands of the Tax Court. So what, I retorted, the laws are as they stand, and if Revcan has led a stealth attack on them over the years then it was up to the courts to bring the situation back in line with the basic tenets of common law. They are just doing their job, he responded. But I pointed out to him that in Scandinavia, where taxes can reach sixty-five percent, the reluctance to pay is low because the taxpayer can see value for money. In our society, where the average taxpayer pays in excess of $15,000 and then has to wait six months or more for a heart operation, it is difficult to portray money for service when the average amount spent per taxpayer on health is less than $3,000. My lawyer friend agreed with me that all the tax avoidance he was now helping to curtail was the result of a lack of faith in the government to provide what it promised with our dollars. This makes the collector's job most difficult. A glass of Merlot later, I had him as an advocate of any simplified flat tax system. What were my arguments?

As you have seen, the Byzantine labyrinth that is the Income Tax Act is a fertile ground for abuse of the taxpayer. There is also no doubt that a cadre of people are working feverishly to thwart the Act.

The abuse of taxpayers occurs because there is very little oversight of the CRA. In the eyes of the politicians, it can't be all bad since it supplies the life blood of politics: money. Also, for the politicos, if there is someone you want to pillory, what better device than the Act? It doesn't seem to matter that CRA has been told not to use audits to seek third-party information, pursue high-profile Canadians, or have investigators masquerade as auditors; it is continuing as you read this.

While you are reading this, there will be thousands of people legally moving their assets offshore, structuring tax shelters, and planning avoidance. At the same time, there are greater numbers of people working desperately to forestall them. I don't know about you, but this strikes me as absurd. There has to be a better way. Those people feverishly working at CRA to make the government rich could be better employed making the country rich. Those lawyers desperately working to preserve the wealth of the rich and the corporations could just as easily be working to uphold our civil liberties.

There are any number of changes in our method of taxation that could resolve the problems. As I mentioned at the outset, a system whereby the greatest taxing power occurs close to home at the municipal level would be a step forward. To some extent, we are seeing this as cities are being given a piece of the taxing power. But what would happen if the cities were given the ability to tax directly either income or transactions? As we have seen in the United States, where taxes are not universally identical, people will seek the lowest tax jurisdiction in which to transact business or maintain residence. In Florida, there is no state income tax, so many elderly people who have the luxury of not having to be in a specific location choose to live there. As well, in the years when inheritance tax was onerous in the United States, there were occasions when the ailing wealthy relative would be moved to Canada to expire, a country with no inheritance tax.[34] In Europe, where tax codes are similar but not identical in all the countries of the European Union, companies set up in the lower tax jurisdictions at the expense of the higher ones. As a result, countries such as Ireland are being castigated for drawing away business at the expense of its neighbours by instituting low tax rates. That drawing away has led to a decade of high prosperity in Ireland.

What would happen in Canada if the major taxing

[34] In Canada, inheritance tax is really capital gains tax. You are taxed on the difference in the value of your assets at death compared to their acquisition cost. In the case of the recently arrived American, his asset base cost was as of the day he crossed the border, a cost that would be similar to the value a short time later at death.

power was removed from Ottawa? To begin with, the feds wouldn't have the cash to hand out in equalization payments. Saskatchewan might offer tax breaks significant enough to lure Bombardier or Ford to establish in Moose Jaw rather than in Ontario or Quebec. So instead of the tax revenue being earned in Ontario and handouts to the have-not provinces, they would establish their own tax base. We would have mini-Irelands in Canada. A not-so-frightening thought.

Another improvement would be the elimination of "general coffers," that huge pot of gold into which your tax money is thrown, and the fight begins to see who can improve his portion of that pot. What if, on a federal level, the government levied a health tax, road tax, education tax, each separately itemized on your tax statement? You'd be able to complain to your MP that the defence tax is too high or the health tax too low. Trying to run some of the many scams that our politicians have undertaken in the past would become difficult because the amount left over after collection for specific expenditures would be minimal, and I'm certain that there would be no item on your tax bill for "buddy payments" or "patronage." Of course, that would mean that those cushy jobs of Canada's agent or counsel in New York, Paris, London, and Los Angeles would have to go. These are not embassies but places to park friends and family members at upward of $7 million a year in costs. And where would the Governor General's office find its $100 million a year? Not on your tax statement.

But that would be a creeping change in the system and liable to abuse. We know that the real tax rate in Canada is about forty percent because that is the portion of the gross domestic product spent by the government. That amount of money is raised through various forms of taxation, including income, excise, customs, and other hidden taxes. It was shown some years ago by then Minister of Finance, Edgar Benson, that if Canada had a flat tax of about seventeen percent on gross income there would be an amount collected from personal income tax equivalent to what is currently collected. "How can that be?" you might ask as you consider the roughly thirty-five percent you paid last year. To begin with, everybody would pay the tax. It would be collected off the top. Right at the gross income level. No tax shelters, no write-offs, no deductions. That would mean that Canada's millionaires would pay the same rate as you; the only difference is that they would pay it.[35]

What good would it do to have a tax rate of ninety percent on all taxable incomes over half a million if no one has a taxable income of that amount? Many people could have a gross income of well over that and end up with a taxable income of zero. As well, have you ever considered that having discriminatory tax rates is undemocratic? Why should someone have a better rate than his richer neighbour, especially if his richer compatriot pays nothing in the final instance?

Under such a system, tax lawyers and accountants would disappear, not to mention CRA auditors and investigators. As well, in the parlance of Edgar Benson, the earlier finance minister who wanted to reform the system, "a buck is a buck" — it wouldn't matter how you acquired your

---

[35] I am often amused by stories planted in the press saying that the top ten percent of earners paid the greater proportion of tax collected than the low-income earners. This kind of analysis makes the poor feel better about the horrendous amounts of tax they pay but doesn't take into account the wealthy, who may pay little if any tax.

dollar, be it capital gains, fees, dividends, or salary: it would be taxed at seventeen percent.

There are a number of reasons why we are unlikely to get a rational and fairer tax system. The people who benefit from the current system don't want to see change. The multimillionaires who pay less tax than you do, the trust beneficiaries who pay no tax, the tax lawyers and accountants, not to mention the legions striving at CRA to ensure tax compliance with a complicated system and the continuance of their paycheques, don't want change.

Income tax was a temporary measure instituted during a National Emergency. Like the temporary housing thrown up at the end of World War I in the lanes behind my house, it was to be torn down when normality returned. Now those houses that were built in contravention of the city's housing standards at the end of the Great War for returning veterans have been protected by the Toronto Historical Board and will live on in perpetuity. Temporary emergency measures are seldom well contemplated or executed. They often become permanent when undertaken by government.

Another problem with current income tax is its fragility. It operates as a result of taxpayers' willingness for self-assessment. That willingness is justified to some extent in the taxpayer's mind by his belief that he is receiving a break and that it's the big earners who are really shouldering the load. The tax records do not support this view. In the late 1970s and 1980s, as tax rates went through the roof, rich people or their assets left Canada at the speed of a wire transfer. Opposition MPs warned of an impending tax revolt. My book *Take Your Money and Run* was waved on the floor of the House of Commons as evidence of the start of such a revolt. Tax revolts are not uncommon. The

United States was founded upon such an event. Remember the Boston Tea Party? Tax revolts are feared by government. Loss of the ability to tax makes government irrelevant. Countries new to the taxation systems have chosen the flat tax. Estonia and Slovenia, the wealthiest of the ex-communist countries, adopted flat tax as their system. Now other European countries are looking at it as an alternative to the graduated and complicated systems that have evolved.

Think of the essence of our system. It is built on the concept of the cooperative taxpayer. In other words, a person who is willing to obey both the spirit and the letter of the law. Suppose Canadians decided one day to obey only the letter? What if they didn't fill in all the blanks but just sent in their receipts with a signed form? What if someone went to a tax lawyer and determined which questions on the tax form were irrelevant and made them known? What if, after being completely identified on your tax form by your social insurance number, you just wrote in for questions regarding your date of birth, address, and other trivia "same as last year"? There would be abject terror in the hearts of Revenue Canada employees. Those are just a few quick thoughts on how the system could be sabotaged. I shudder to think what you or other Canadians can conceive of to disrupt the harvest.

The tax collectors are also setting themselves up for a potential disaster as they try to trim collection costs by moving to electronic filing. The mayhem that could occur if someone became malicious with that system is terrifying. What was hated in the military was the barrack room lawyer. Imagine a country where that sort of thing is common. In Alberta, there are people who have actually read the Constitution Act, 1867, and 1982, and the BNA Act. Their knowledge of those acts combined with the computing skills present in the oil province must keep a few people awake in Ottawa at night. But what happens when the oil patch makes an instant multimillionaire? Usually, a plane ticket to a tax haven is sold.

In the case of Canada's fleeing millionaires, there wasn't as much angst in the capital with regard to their flight compared with what would happen if the equity of the tax system became a consideration of the vast source of funding known as the middle class. When reports of upper-middle-class members of our society shipping their assets offshore surfaced, the government sprang into overdrive. All sorts of new reporting requirements and privacy invasions were undertaken. Note how nothing happened to stop the upper classes. After all, they were a minor part of the tax pie. Without the compliance of the middle-class taxpayer, the system collapses because the cost of collection rises. There are myriad ways that the middle class could stage a revolt over income tax rather than just voting with their feet or moving their assets. The ability to stage a revolt on a system where the flat rate is collected similarly to the GST makes disobedience nearly impossible.

CHAPTER 22

Tax on the BARREL HEAD

GETTING TO LOVE THE VAT

Will we ever have a flat tax? If we follow the European path, we will get there by default rather than by plan. In Europe, where taxation has been under attack since before the Duke of Alba hung reluctant payers, the countries are moving more to consumption taxes. Thus, "value-added tax" or VAT rates have been creeping up, while the amounts collected under income tax have fallen. In Greece, if you buy an expensive car, boat, or house, the taxman is advised, and you receive a visit from the income tax guys, who then negotiate a higher annual tax to be paid. Although your tax form may not indicate it, your lifestyle certainly shows that you are a person of some substance and hence liable to higher tax. Can you imagine the inefficiency?

People who attack the consumption or VAT tax systems base their assault on the belief that the rich won't pay their fair share. I look at it from what some people advocate for drunk drivers — confiscate their cars. In that way, the wealthy are penalized proportionally to the poor. The same with VAT. Can you imagine Conrad Black arriving at his $35 million London digs in a Honda Civic? No, in spite of having to pay an extra nineteen percent (the rate in some European countries), he will still purchase the Rolls-Royce. Other VAT bashers mention the difficulties for government when the economy slows and the amount of VAT collected at the cash register declines as well. This makes the funding of expanded government spending difficult during recessions. Well, how about this? Let's inform the citizenry that the VAT rate will be halved as a result of recession for one year, but only for that year. Can you imagine the stimulus to the economy as everyone dashes out to take advantage of the tax break?

Others complain that VAT is regressive in that it falls more heavily on the poor than on the rich. To ease the burden on the poor under current income tax systems, we have minimum thresholds that must be earned before incurring tax. Have you ever noticed how those levels are never as high as the official poverty level? At the time of this writing, once you passed $9,000, you started paying income tax, while the poverty level is set at over $20,000. Something is wrong there. How do we provide the same protection or better under VAT? Food, medical expenses, and pharmaceuticals are made exempt. But now we are getting back into the complexity of the income tax system. What about lobsters, filet mignons, and exotic cheeses? Did you know that if you buy salted cashew nuts you pay

GST because they are considered a prepared meal, while the unsalted nuts are considered food? Of course, the next question is how much salt constitutes salted? Oh, oh, I can see the tax code expanding. So let's re-examine the flat tax.

When there are no deductions, loopholes, or write-offs, what is a poor auditor to do? Unless you falsify your reported income, there is only one gross figure: the sum of all that you earned in a year. Ah, yes, you say, but what about all those perks? You know, the free vacation ("junket" in political terms), the company car, the use of the ski chalet, and other little benefits. They're all part of your income, and the same rules would apply to the politicians. Oh, oh, I can see the flat tax fading away. But what would happen if our closest neighbour adopts a flat tax? Impossible, you say. In truth, the United States is slipping into a flat tax as I write this.

Many years ago, to ensure that everyone paid something, the United States instituted a tax that required people to pay, although they took advantage of enough loopholes to reduce their income to a nontaxable level. This alternative minimum tax imposed a threshold of gross income above which you were taxable regardless of whatever tax breaks you might adopt. The tax rate was a flat rate regardless of the amount of your gross income. Interestingly, 3.5 million U.S. taxpayers were caught in the minimum tax in 2003, 19 million in 2004, and the number is expected to double within five years. Without legislative changes, the United States will be a flat tax country. What, then, for Canada?

The clarity and predictability of tax liabilities would certainly encourage high-income Canadians to pursue their careers in the United States versus Canada. Who are those high-income earners? They are the entrepreneurs and visionaries who expand the economy. They are the technocrats who grease the economy's wheels. You could witness in Canada what Europe has seen with the flight of high earners to Ireland, leaving us without the people necessary to expand our economy.

We desperately need change. Ah, you say, you can't change the system because you can't fight city hall. Not true. I literally did fight city hall and won. It's called civil disobedience, and it works. David Thoreau wrote about it, and Gandhi and I practised it. There have been tax revolts throughout history. Charles Adams in his book *For Good and Evil* describes the history of taxation. After reading that book, I couldn't help but conclude that income tax as we know it is probably the worst form of taxation for the citizen. Not for the taxpayer, but for the citizen.

Income tax as it is practised in North America is deceptive, discriminatory, and abusive. It has been cobbled together from an impromptu temporary system because government was reluctant to let it go. I doubt that the employees of CRA want to lie to and harass people, but the system forces them into that kind of behaviour because it is deceptive.

In 1969, there was an examination of our tax system, and it was found lacking. Some concrete measures, such as a flat tax on all forms of income, were recommended. It is a sad statement on the calibre of people in government at that time that they couldn't accept the recommendations of their own experts. There were also the legions of tax lawyers and accountants who would have had their golden calves gored. They certainly opposed the changes. I doubt that any of the upper echelon of Revcan would have been receptive to a tax system that would eliminate their departments and jobs.

If we get forced into a form of flat tax or consumption

tax by stealth, then we will continue to have an unruly tax monster. If we get forced into a tax system as a result of taxpayer anger, it will once more be a compromise. The proper course would be a complete revamping and the establishment of a simple and fair tax system. We don't have representative government in Canada; we have responsible government. If our government is truly responsible, then it has to accept the blame for the state of our tax system, and it is up to government to take the responsibility to reform it.